THE HEALING GARDEN

THE HEALING GARDEN

gardening for the mind, body and soul

GAY SEARCH

Photography by Jonathan Buckley

BBC

The Healing Garden was first broadcast in 2001 as part of *Gardeners' World*, which is produced by Catalyst Television for the BBC.

Published by BBC Worldwide Ltd, Woodlands, 80 Wood Lane, London W12 OTT

First published 2001
© Gay Search 2001
The moral right of the author has been asserted.

Photography © Jonathan Buckley 2001

ISBN 0 563 53704 3

Commissioning Editor: Nicky Copeland
Project Editor: Sarah Miles
Copy Editor: Christine King
Cover Art Director: Pene Parker
Book Art Director: Lisa Pettibone
Designer: Liz Hallam
Picture Researcher: Bea Thomas

Set in Adobe Garamond and Foundry Sans
Printed and bound in Italy by Chromo Litho Ltd
Colour separations by Kestrel Digital Colour, Chelmsford

Above: *Ilex aquifolium* 'J. C. van Tol'
Above far right: *Eccremocarpus scaber*

CONTENTS

Introduction

If you are a gardener then you will have no doubt that your garden makes you feel good. It gives you enormous pleasure and a great sense of satisfaction – indeed, a recent survey showed not only that 51 per cent of men questioned preferred gardening to going to the pub or playing sport, but also that 25 per cent of the women preferred gardening to sex! When you come in from a good afternoon's gardening you may feel tired, but it's the right kind of tired – the kind that comes from physical work well done in the fresh air and in beautiful surroundings, not the kind that comes after a string of stressful meetings and a nightmare journey home.

While you know that gardening and your garden make you feel good, you may not know that they also positively *do* you good. What *The Healing Garden* sets out to do is show you how your garden can be an even more valuable resource for your health and well-being – physically, mentally and spiritually. If you have a garden, but don't yet think of yourself as a gardener, then *The Healing Garden* hopes to show you how even an ordinary small backyard can be made into a beautiful and practical healing garden, and convince you to give gardening a try.

With the help of designer Jean Goldberry, we turned a typical, small garden into a healing garden, incorporating as many elements as the 10 × 5m (33 × 16ft) space would allow. While I'm not suggesting you should rethink your whole garden along these lines, there may be ideas that you could adapt to suit your own plot, because it is certainly well worth doing.

Gardens and plants in themselves are good for our health. Trees are the lungs of our polluted cities, converting carbon dioxide into oxygen. They also take up and filter out a number of other serious pollu-

tants in the atmosphere as well as protecting us from solar radiation, which is why the British National Urban Forestry Unit is campaigning so hard to increase the number of trees in our towns and cities. You can do your bit for your own sake and for the wider community by planting suitable trees and shrubs in your garden.

You can also improve your health by growing some of your own food, especially if you grow it organically. Despite one recent study that suggested there are no benefits in eating organic produce, many people dislike the idea of ingesting quantities of pesticides and herbicides. And at least if they grow their own, they know it hasn't been genetically modified, and nobody would deny that eating a lettuce that was picked five minutes ago is healthier than eating one picked last week, chilled and flown half-way around the world. There is something enormously

Left: *Aconitum* 'Newry Blue'

satisfying, elemental almost, about feeding yourself in part at least from your own plot, and the fruits of your own labour will, I guarantee, taste better than any others you have ever eaten. You don't need a huge amount of space either. Even in the smallest garden you can find room, not only for vegetables, grown in containers if necessary or in a border in among other plants, but also for fruit, grown flat against walls or fences.

Your garden can also be your pharmacy. For many thousands of years, plants have been used for medicinal purposes, and though herbal medicine has been out of favour in the West for the last two hundred years, there is a growing revival of interest in it and other complementary therapies – aromatherapy, for example, and flower remedies. It's partly that we are becoming concerned about the side-effects of drugs, partly that we want to take more responsibility for our own health and

partly that we are more interested in a holistic approach to our health and ourselves, understanding that mind, body and spirit are inextricably linked. So rather than take indigestion tablets, pick a handful of mint and make peppermint tea. Or, if you're finding it hard to sleep, try chamomile tea or lavender oil on your pillow last thing at night.

Gardening as an activity is also very good for you physically. It's a valuable form of exercise, provided – as with any other form of exercise – you don't go at it like a bull at a gate. It works all the main muscle groups and also gives your heart and lungs a good workout. Did you know that men and women both burn more calories per minute digging or hedge trimming than they do cycling and only slightly fewer than they do swimming? And unlike other forms of exercise which are an end in themselves and so can become boring very quickly, gardening has

Below: After just three months the healing garden has become a much-used, and enjoyed, space.

a tangible end product – a beautiful garden and delicious home-grown produce – as well as benefits to health.

The Green Gym project, organized jointly by a health centre in Sonning Common, Berkshire, and the British Trust for Conservation Volunteers in 1998 involved a number of mainly older people in gardening tasks – clearing ground, digging, raking, hedge-trimming, planting and so forth – but in the context of conservation projects in the countryside. Veronica Reynolds of Oxford Brookes University evaluated the effect on their health and general well-being. The heart rate of one forty-year-old woman who took part in the Green Gym and also did a step aerobics class once a week was measured during both activities. It showed not only that she expended more energy in the Green Gym, but also that she spent longer in the 'training zone' where the cardiovascular system really benefits.

Overall, the quality of life – including mental as well as physical health – improved for the volunteers and other Green Gym projects are being set up around Britain. The study suggests that a factor may have been 'biophilia'. This is the idea that we have a biologically based attraction to nature, and that our quality of life in the broadest sense depends on the extent to which we are plugged into the natural world. It's interesting that when people are learning relaxation techniques that involve visualization, the place they most often conjure up is a garden or the countryside. Some choose the seaside initially, but don't stay with it for long, while those who choose a garden do.

Gardening is therapy and one of the best stress-busters there is. Getting out into the garden after a hard day at the office and pottering for an hour, or even just sitting there and looking around, is an ideal way to unwind. It's wholly absorbing – any

gardener who says she or he has never gone out into the garden and lost all track of time is either being economical with the truth or is not a real gardener – a largely stress-free activity that forces you to slow down to the pace of the natural world, the pace at which we all lived until very recently in our history. Being in a garden, surrounded by beautiful plants, calms the mind, soothes and lifts the spirit.

What we hope *The Healing Garden* will do is convince you of the many benefits to be had and inspire you to turn at least part of your plot into a healing garden of your own.

gay search

The designer's plan of the healing garden (opposite) and the overview (above), show how many different areas can be included in an average-sized garden.

Gardens of the mind and spirit

To say 'gardening is the best therapy there is' has become a cliché but, like most clichés, it has become one because it is true. So many gardeners will tell you that whatever the stresses and strains of the day, there are very few problems that an hour or two pottering in the garden won't at least put into perspective. And while some Japanese companies have rooms with a model of the boss that frustrated employees can attack, gardeners find some vigorous digging with a good sharp spade and bit of imagination can have a very similar effect.

Bud of *Magnolia* × *soulangeana* 'Lennei'

How many of us nip out into the garden for just ten minutes and find suddenly that several hours have passed, the kids haven't had their tea and that it's almost dark? Gardening is one of the best antidotes to stress there is. Some stress is good for us. It triggers the 'fight or flight' mechanism, which gives us that essential rush of adrenaline and other hormones to speed up our metabolism and produce additional insulin, cholesterol and blood sugar in order to cope with danger or excitement. Originally all the excess would be used up in the physical action that followed – fight or flight. But these days most adrenaline-producing situations are not physically dangerous, nor are they resolved by physical action, and the fact that many of us are under stress for a long period is something our metabolism was simply not designed to cope with. So our metabolism is fighting back and stress is at the root of many modern illnesses. According to the British Health and Safety Executive, it is the cause of 6.5 million lost working days each year.

Gardens and gardening counter stress in a number of ways. Just being in a garden or green space reduces stress levels. Work done in the USA by Professor Roger Ulrich over the last twenty years has proved this time and time again. One of his studies took two groups of patients who had just had gall bladder operations. One group of twenty-three patients was put in rooms overlooking trees, while the other twenty-three matched patients were put in rooms overlooking buildings. The tree group recovered quicker, went home sooner, needed less pain relief and also complained less.

In other experiments, Professor Ulrich exposed people to stress by showing them anxiety-inducing videos or simulated stressful car journeys, and then took them to green and leafy places. Their blood pressure, brain activity and muscle tension were monitored throughout, and the experiments all show that within as little as three minutes of being surrounded by greenery, there was a measurable reduction in the symptoms of stress. Just sitting in the garden at the end of a long hard day, or even in the park for ten minutes at lunchtime, is a great way to counteract stress.

The act of gardening itself is very beneficial, too. First, it is physical activity, something that many of who spend our lives at desks or in cars or slumped in front of the television badly need. Many of us work with our brains all day, and just getting out into the garden and doing simple manual tasks – weeding, mowing the lawn, deadheading, watering – helps us switch off. Other tasks demanding more skill and concentration, such as pricking out seedlings or pruning a rose, are also a valuable diversion. At a time when so many of us do little else with our hands other than tap at a keyboard all day long, practising manual skills – becoming good at them, taking pride in them – offers a sense of satisfaction. And while we may not be conscious of it, there is something

The new frond of a tree fern unfurling in spring is a fresh and vibrant symbol of hope and renewal.

almost elemental about doing the same jobs, with very similar tools, that our ancestors have done for thousands of years. A spade, albeit stainless steel or Teflon-coated, is still a spade, and it's highly unlikely that anyone will ever invent an electronic deadheading machine.

For the vast majority of our time on Earth as a species, we lived off the land. It's only in the last two hundred years that most of us have become urban dwellers, divorced from the land and from nature, but the need to be in touch with the soil hasn't been bred out of us in what is, in evolutionary terms, a very short time.

Most of us live our lives at breakneck pace. The Internet means that much of our working lives happens in a heartbeat: no longer do we have the breathing space between the letter posted and the reply, or even between the time it takes to receive a fax, read it, then type out and send an answer. We can prepare a whole hot meal in three minutes – or less if your micro-wave is even more powerful. We can do the shopping at 3 o'clock on a Sunday morning if we choose to. There is prac-tically no down time any more.

But there is in gardening. Gardening slows us down. No matter how important you are or how much money you have, the first snowdrops will appear only when they are ready to, the shrub will grow only as fast as optimum conditions will allow, the leaves will fall off the trees when the time is right. Gardening works in its own time frame, nature's time frame, and when you garden you have no choice but to slow down to its pace. Gardening teaches us patience, and while it's possible to have an instant buzz, it also teaches us to delay gratification – a valuable lesson at a time when we all expect to have what we want *now*. When you plant, say, *Paeonia mlokosewitschii* and wait four years for it to produce its first flower, by golly do you enjoy it when it does appear! And the fact that its beauty is only fleeting adds to the

A simple seat enclosed by a curtain of weeping willow branches provides a relaxing space in which to sit and contemplate the still, reflective surface of the pond.

intensity of the experience.

In centrally heated homes, and air-conditioned offices, and with strawberries available in the supermarket 363 days a year (they do close on Christmas Day and Easter Sunday), we tend to lose track of the seasons. Gardening brings you directly back into contact with the yearly cycle – really the only activity in modern life that still does. It has an inevitability that is reassuring. No matter how bad the winter, you know that spring will come. As the actor Michael Caine once said, when the first daffodil appears after an English winter you feel you've bloody well deserved it!

When you garden you notice the subtle seasonal changes – the buds beginning to swell when it still feels like winter, the first leaves turning colour on a hot summer day – and you cannot but be aware of the cycle of life.

You can't fail to be aware either that this cycle goes on regardless of our efforts. You can help, you can encourage, you can pro-tect and nurture, but beyond that plants do their own thing. Plants were here long before we were and will be here long after we have gone. You need only look at buildings that become derelict. It takes very little time for the plants and wildlife to come back and take over.

You may think you've imposed your will on the garden, but then plants don't do as you expect. They don't stay where you've put them, and suddenly pop up somewhere else, creating a spectacular combination that you would never have thought of. They are earlier or later in flower than they were the previous year, thereby missing that clever combination you'd planned, or, having thrived for many seasons, they suddenly give up the ghost. Plants that you didn't put there appear in your garden – nuts buried by squirrels perhaps, or seeds dropped by birds. Control freaks may find this deeply frustrating, but then not many control freaks garden, probably for that very reason.

Autumn mists in the Valley Gardens in Windsor Great Park show that every season has its own particular pleasures and make us more aware of the yearly cycle.

The United Nations declared in 1982 that 'living in harmony with nature gives man the best opportunities for the development of his creativity and for rest and recreation'. Most gardeners come to appreciate the benefits that come with being a part of nature, of working with it, rather than fighting an inevitably losing battle against it. After all, it is far more stressful being a lord of creation rather than just one small element in it. Sharing your garden with wildlife brings much more satisfaction than defending your territory against it. There is great pleasure to be had in seeing and hearing birds in the garden, so grow plants with berries and seeds that provide them with food and others that will offer them shelter. On a purely practical level, they will also repay your hospitality by eating many garden pests. Grow plants that will attract butterflies into your garden, just for the sheer pleasure of looking at their extraordinary intricate beauty.

At a time when there is so much concern about environmental issues, from GMOs to the continued erosion of the countryside – hundreds of acres go under concrete every year – many people feel concerned but powerless, a state that contributes to depression. In that regard, gardening is very empowering, because it gives you the opportunity to do something about it. You can make your garden a haven for wildlife, driven out of the countryside by modern farming methods and development. You can also grow some of your own food, and by gardening in a sustainable and organic way you can do your bit to keep the land in good heart to hand on to the next generation. If you want yours to be a healing garden, you won't want to smother it in chemicals, thereby disturbing the balance of the natural world. By gardening organically you will encourage natural predators such as birds, ladybirds and lacewings, that will keep down common pests – greenfly, slugs, snails and so forth.

Gardening is also creative. It gives people who feel they have no artistic talent for, say, painting or drawing an opportunity to create something visually beautiful. For people who work primarily with the organizational, structured, mathematical left side of the brain, the chance to use the more intuitive, artistic right side is important in creating balance.

Gardening is essentially an optimistic activity. By definition, planting or sowing anything is investing in the future, and gardeners are always thinking ahead, looking forward. Gardening also gives you endless second chances. Okay, so something didn't work quite as well this summer as you had hoped. Never mind. There's always next year, another opportunity to try again, to do better, though unless something truly catastrophic has hit your garden – a very late frost, or extensive drifting weedkiller damage – you will still have had a good enough display or crop to give you pleasure and satisfaction.

It's for reasons such as this that horticultural therapy is so valuable for people suffering from mental illness or learning difficulties. Thrive, the charity formerly known as Horticultural Therapy, is involved with some 1500 therapeutic projects up and down Britain, some large, some small. The Blackwater Gardens in Barming near Maidstone was started by a doctor eight years ago in part as a response to patients who would come back to him again and again with chronic problems for which he had no solution. He decided to try – if you like – prescribing gardening. Now sixty to seventy patients work in the beautiful acre and a half garden, growing organic vegetables for the café, which is open to the public every day, and other plants. Graham Carpenter, who is in

Plants like *Sedum* 'Autumn Joy' are not only beautiful in their own right but are a magnet for butterflies which bring their own beauty into the garden.

Water plays a vital role in the Islamic-influenced gardens at the Alhambra in Granada, Spain, both in the long straight canals and in the narrow jets of water arching high over them.

charge of the gardens and greenhouse, believes that working in a natural environment, having physical contact with the soil, is a literally grounding experience for people who are mentally ill. The fact that the garden and its surroundings are beautiful is also very important in feeding the spirit.

Growing plants also offers a relationship with something living, an opportunity to be nurturing, to feel needed, without the pressures or guilt involved in relationships with other people or even pets. As the American playwright Arthur Miller put it, 'Whenever life seems pointless and difficult to grasp, you can always get out in the garden and get something done. Also, your paternal or maternal instincts come into play because helpless living things are depending on you, requiring training and encouragement, and protection from enemies.' Unlike children, plants won't want to borrow the car, tap you for money, or treat the place like a hotel!

There is also immense satisfaction to be had from, say, seeing seeds that you have sown germinate and grow into plants. It's a validation, a feeling that you can't be all bad if plants will grow for you, which is very important to people who suffer from low self-esteem, who always associate themselves with failure, whether they are mentally ill or not.

SPIRITUAL GARDENS

As well as providing solace and stimulation for the mind, gardens have always had an important spiritual dimension. Even people who are not religious in a conventional sense cannot but be aware of some greater power at work when they look at plants. I often say jokingly that daffodils must have been designed by a Swede, because there is something so clean and

modern about the shape of the trumpet and that clear primary yellow. The more you examine plants, the more the extraordinary, precise nature of their forms and patterns emerges. In the thirteenth century in Pisa, the mathematician Leonardo Fibonacci discovered a sequence of numbers – 1, 1, 2, 3, 5, 8, 13, 21, 34, 55 and so on – achieved by adding each number to the one before it. He found these numbers occur in nature, in seashells, in the family tree of bees, and in plants (before the modern hybridists got at them, that is). The numbers of petals on a flower, or of seeds in a seedhead – whether it's a sunflower or pine cone – or of leaves along a stem are Fibonacci numbers. Members of the aster family, for example, have either thirty-four or fifty-five petals. And if you count the seeds in a sunflower seedhead, starting at the centre and counting in spirals to the left and to the right, you will find they too are Fibonacci numbers. It does seem very unlikely, doesn't it, that all this is purely random?

Right from the earliest times, it is probable that gardens have had a religious or spiritual dimension. Martin Palmer and David Manning suggest in their book *Sacred Gardens* that once people began to settle in communities rather than being hunter-gatherers, 'perhaps a new and deeper understanding of nature as the face of the Divine emerged. If so – and the Bible and other ancient holy books do indicate this – then one response was to create gardens. It is not too strong a statement to say that the creation of the garden was an expression of a new relationship with both nature and the divine.'

Certainly all the great early civilizations had gardens. In ancient Egypt, the earliest surviving garden plan dates from 1400 BC, but is so sophisticated in its design – with a long pergola, a symmetrical layout but divided into 'rooms' so that the overall design would not be obvious when you were in it – that it suggests it was the culmination of a long period of development rather than a first attempt. Priests had gardens attached to the temples, probably for growing plants used in rituals but, given the Egyptian love and reverence for nature, also for spiritual purposes.

The idea of the garden as paradise is a very early one, too, far earlier than the Bible. In fact the word doesn't appear in the Bible until the Greeks translated it from the Hebrew in the second century AD. The word comes from *pairidaeza*, a word in the ancient Persian religious language, Zend, meaning an enclosure or walled garden. These gardens were created in the middle of baking hot cities or on the edge of the desert as sanctuaries, retreats from a hostile environment and a place to refresh body and soul. Water was a vital element, not only for its cooling effect but

for its symbolic meaning as the source of all life. There were often four channels from the central pool – the wellspring of life – dividing the garden into four, since the Persians believed that the universe was divided into four quarters.

Later, when the Arabs conquered Persia in AD 637, they took over the basic idea of the paradise garden – essential in their climate – and refined it. Their love of mathematics, and the fact that the Koran forbids the making of any image in human or animal form, led them to value geometric patterns, resulting in some of the exquisite tiled courtyard gardens that still survive in North Africa and Spain.

Gardens were central to the religion of Islam and appear often in the Koran: 'Allah has promised to believers, men and women, Gardens under which rivers flow, and here they will dwell in beautiful mansions in gardens of everlasting bliss.' The Islamic paradise is a garden, and gardens on Earth are a reflection, a foretaste of what is to come in the afterlife, and they are a joint venture between God and humanity. In Islamic teaching, we have been appointed God's khalifa – or deputy – to rule over the whole of creation but, far from exploiting our position, we are expected to care for all the living things that share the Earth with us as we would care for ourselves. No garden would be considered a proper garden in Islam unless it had birds, bees, butterflies, even fish in the ponds. 'If anyone plants a tree or sows the land,' wrote the prophet Mohammed, 'and people, beasts or birds eat from it, he should consider it as a charity on his part.'

Water remained vital – for practical as well as symbolic purposes. There was always a central pool or canal, usually still and unplanted to reflect the sky and also to symbolize the fact that the garden is a reflection of paradise. The sound of water was important too, so fountains were often

An ancient Egyptian mural of a garden with a very well stocked pond.

included. Not only is the sound of gentle splashing calming and a diversion from distracting noises of the world outside, the droplets of water in the air also help to cool it down. One of the most famous surviving Islamic gardens, the Alhambra in Granada, Spain, has long canals with rows of jets on either side, sending the water in slender arcs over the canal before splashing gently into it.

There were channels of water too dividing up the garden, often tiled to make what was very shallow water (since water was so scarce in that climate) look deeper, because of the Islamic belief that paradise was divided by four rivers. These canals flow north, south, east and west, taking the eye, the mind and the spirit from the inner world of the garden into the greater world outside.

The plants chosen were often those mentioned in the Koran as growing in paradise – fruit and nut trees such as almonds, apples, oranges, and peaches – which are also rich in symbolism. Orange trees symbolize life and bitter Morello cherries the fruits of the soul, while tall narrow cypresses symbolize both eternal life and death. Roses were also very important in Persian and Islamic gardens for their beauty, their fragrance and symbolism. In Islamic legend, the first rose was created from a drop of sweat falling from Mohammed's brow. In Persian legend, the rose was created in the Great Garden of Persia by the first rays of the rising sun, and when a soul knocked on the door of the next world to seek admittance, the only material thing allowed to cross the threshold was a red rose.

As the Arabs conquered parts of Asia, North Africa and Spain, during the sixth and seventh centuries AD, they took their gardens with them. In India, gardens around temples and tombs were already similar in many ways – walled, symmetrical, with water (symbolic as well as practical for worshippers to cleanse themselves before worship) – and the styles merged. Much later, between the thirteenth and sixteenth centuries, the Moguls in India brought the symbol of the octagon into garden design. An octagon consists of two squares, laid one on top of the other to make a stylized circle. The square represents humanity, and the circle the oneness of God. The two combined are the perfect symbol for a garden.

While the private houses and public arenas of ancient Greece and Rome had their gardens, these were relatively simple until the influence of the ornate pleasure gardens of the East arrived in the third century BC, and had no spiritual purpose. For that, there was the sacred grove, often the remnant of ancient forest, dedicated to a god, often Diana goddess of hunting. It was thought to be the home of deities, a place where rituals were performed, but it was also a wilderness, nature in the raw, the antithesis to 'civilization'.

Sacred groves appear in many other cultures. In India, for instance, the groves sacred to the god Krishna near his birthplace in northern India have been worshipped for possibly thousands of years, and are currently being restored. In Celtic Britain, too, there were many sacred groves.

By the early Iron Age, half of England – some estimates suggest up to two-thirds – had ceased to be wild wood, so that when the Romans arrived Britain was not greatly more wooded than it is today. Certainly, by the time they left, their intensive farming practices had left great tracts of England almost bare of trees. In response to this increasingly controlled landscape, the Celts deemed the wild places of bogs, woods, springs, trees and rivers to be sacred, and rituals, which took place in clearings within the sacred grove, celebrated the untamed power of nature. Some of these groves still

Roses were important symbolically in Persian and Islamic gardens.

Right: This is a New York recreation of a mediaeval cloister garden. While it has far more plants that the original garth, it gives a very clear sense of how the green centre glimpsed from the shadows would aid contemplation.

survive today, such as Wanelund Wood in Norfolk ('Lúndr' being the Old Norse word for sacred grove).

When the Romans invaded Britain in 55 BC, they brought their gardens with them. Gardens had been very important to the Romans. The rich had splendid villa gardens enclosed by walls in towns and by hedges in the countryside. They were rectangular and all the lines within them were either straight or – if they curved – they were perfect arcs. There was usually a terrace linking house and garden with a pergola of climbing plants, often vines, and they were filled with statuary. Even the less wealthy had small gardens, an area of greenery, often plants growing in pots and usually edible.

By the fourth century AD, the arrival of Christianity in Britain led to the development of monastic gardens, which combined the formal layout of the Roman model with the practical and spiritual needs of Christianity. For the monks and nuns who made and cared for them, these gardens were an opportunity to create paradise in miniature, with God, nature and humanity all united in a common purpose. The gardens were rich in symbolism, with many plants having a religious significance as their common names reveal. The Madonna lily, for example, named after the Virgin Mary, is a symbol of purity and holiness, as is the white rose. The common names of many plants are contractions of Our Lady – lady's mantle (*Alchemilla mollis*), for example, and lady's bedstraw (*Galium verum*). Others are named after saints: St Bernard's lily (*Anthericum liliago*), St Dabeoc's heath (*Daboecia cantabrica*), and St John's wort (*Hypericum perforatum*) – named for John the Baptist not only because it exudes a red pigment which is symbolic of the blood spilt when he was beheaded, but because it flowers at Midsummer on his feast day. The clover

leaf, St Patrick believed, was a symbol of the Holy Trinity – each leaflet separate and equal but making a whole. Angelica – its full botanical name is *Angelica archangelica* just in case anyone misses the point – was thought to be a gift from heaven.

Monastery gardens were carefully sited, as was the monastery itself, with the church, its spiritual heart, facing towards the East, towards Jerusalem the Holy City, and the rising sun, which symbolizes the Resurrection and the renewal of life. The gardens – for there were several of them – were placed around it. The herb garden, for instance, was usually sited to the north, and near the infirmary. In the East, the most sacred orientation, the flower garden was under the charge of the sacristan. He was the monk in charge of sacred objects and was also responsible for decorating the high altar, the most sacred place in the church, with flowers – some of the most beautiful objects in creation.

As for contemplation, there was always a cloister garth – a rectangle of smooth, plain green turf, usually in the centre of the cloisters, around which the monks processed several times a day. It was often divided into four, just like Roman gardens and indeed Persian and Islamic gardens before them. There may have been water, too, to aid contemplation but nothing else. Green, as we know, is an ideal colour for meditation and, protected from the bustle of the world outside by the cloisters, the calm and peaceful atmosphere created in the cloister garth was perfect for contemplation. The very simplicity and emptiness at the heart of the garth reflected the ultimate aim of contemplation – to move beyond the material, beyond words, beyond self into what author Martin Palmer calls the Divine Emptiness. While we may not be in search of such a profound spiritual experience, just sitting in a quiet area of the garden

Even in the smallest city garden greenery and water create an ideal spot for contemplation.

A buddha surrounded
by contrasting foliage
and smooth pebbles
makes a simple shrine.

surrounded by greenery can very quickly
help us feel at peace with the world and
with ourselves.

CHINESE TAOIST GARDENS

Although different in many ways to western gardens, the gardens of China (and
Japan too) have a similar spiritual goal –
to help people through contemplation
ultimately achieve a state of divine emptiness, or 'no mind' as it's called in Taoism.

In China from the sixth century BC,
the Tao, or the Way, was the main religion
which believed in the One, a mysterious
universal spirit that permeates and
energizes the whole cosmos and everything
in it. It looked to nature for its inspiration
and saw humanity as just one part of the
whole – a philosophy clearly seen in Taoist
gardens. According to an ancient Taoist
saying, 'A garden that does not yield to
hills, streams and ancient trees but is all
the work of humanity, cannot possibly be
of interest. The wonder of the garden is in
the use of the scenery, not in the creation

of it.' Nature knows best, and our role is
simply to enhance it, not try to improve
on it. We should learn from it, and try to
model our behaviour on its effortless spon-
taneity. Gardens must respond to the
essential, innate nature of the landscape
around them, of trees and plants, water,
rock and stone. There is nothing neat or
symmetrical or manufactured about the
Taoist garden.

Space, emptiness, is a part of nature and
what is not there should be as important a
part of the garden as what is. The *Tao Te
Ching*, a fourth-century BC text, says,
'If you mould a cup, you have to make a
hollow: it is the emptiness within it that
makes it useful.'

Yin and yang

Another very important principle in Taoism is Yin and Yang – the two counterbal-
anced, elemental forces in the cosmos. As
the Yellow Emperor Huang Ti wrote in his
book on medicine in the third millennium
BC, 'The principle of yin and yang is the
basic principle of the entire universe. It is
the principle of everything in creation.'
These forces are totally opposed to each
other, but because each one contains the
germ of the other – the small spots of the
opposite tone in the famous black and
white tai ch'i symbol – neither one can be
victorious over the other. They are morally
neutral, neither good nor evil, nor are they
divine forces. They just describe the way
things are. Although all living things contain both, most things are predominantly
one or the other.

Yin represents, primarily, the female:
cold, smooth, soft, still water, tranquil,
winter, the north, night, valleys and the
Earth.

Yang represents male: hot, hard, jagged,
dry, fast-flowing water, active, summer, the
south, day, mountains and Heaven.

In an ideal world, Yin and Yang always

balance each other – night follows day follows night, winter follows summer follows winter (via spring and autumn), there is the right amount of heat and cool-ness, of water and drought and so on. When they are out of balance, misfortune will follow.

Our role in the cosmos – and in the garden – is to maintain the balance between the two, and the way to achieve that is with feng shui.

Feng shui

Feng shui has become extremely popular in the West in recent years. There are books and even magazines devoted to it. People talk about 'the relationship corner' and the importance of keeping the loo seat down so that wealth cannot escape that way. While the more hard-headed among us may view it with a certain degree of scepticism, it is worth remembering that this ancient Chinese system of thought is still used in Hong Kong and indeed all

over China by giant corporations – not known for being off with the fairies – when they are planning and building multi-million-dollar projects.

No one knows exactly when feng shui developed in China but it was several thousand years ago. It started essentially as a town planning tool. A feng shui master would seek out the most auspicious site for a new village by finding a place with the best possible energy or life breath, known as qi or ch'i, flowing through it. It would be a spot that was a little bit warmer than most in winter and a little bit cooler in summer. It would probably be on a gentle slope, protected at the back from north winds, with a sunny open aspect at the front, water nearby and fertile soil. There is a lot in feng shui that is just plain com-mon sense.

Feng shui, which means 'wind water', is concerned with the way we interact with our environment. While many people in the West think of it in relation to the

Flowing water, amid carefully sited rocks on a carpet of moss-like Mind-your-own-business (*Soleirolia soleirolii*), creates the essence of a Japanese garden.

An area where Wood dominates, in the rectangular shapes of the pergola, in the colour green and of course in the wood itself. There is a touch of Earth in the terracotta pots.

correct balance between hard and soft, wet and dry, hot and cold, Earth and Heaven – perpendicular and horizontal in other words – and so on.

Five Elements

Another underlying principle of feng shui, which is also present in Chinese medicine, is the Five Elements – fire, earth, metal, water and wood. It is through these that qi manifests itself, both literally and symbolically.

FIRE

Its season: summer. Its shape: triangular – mountains or roofs. Hot colours. Yin colour: red/purple. Yang colour: sky blue. (This may seem odd at first, but if you look at a flame you will see that it has a lot of blue in it.) In the garden: hot colours, and triangular shapes such as obelisks. Appears as itself in barbecues, chimeneas and candles.

EARTH

Its season: early autumn. Its shape: square. Earthy colours. Yin colour: yellow. Yang colour: brick red, brown. In the garden: soil (obviously), terracotta and ceramic pots and tiles.

METAL

Its season: autumn. Its shape: round, curved. Metallic colours. Yin colours: bronze and silver. Yang colours: white and gold. In the garden: furniture and structures, round ornaments, metallic planting such as *Carex comans* bronze and *Acaena* 'Copper Carpet'.

WATER

Its season: winter. Its shape: wavy or horizontal. Water colours. Yin colour: dark blue. Yang colour: black. In the garden: water features, horizontal or trailing plants.

interior of their home, the outside is far more important. About 70 per cent of what matters in feng shui is location – because it is essentially about helping us to live in balance with nature.

It takes as its starting point the belief shared by all Chinese philosophies that there is qi or ch'i flowing through all living and inanimate things, including ourselves and our environment, and that it is blockages to the flow of qi that create problems with our health, success and happiness. Its aim, therefore, is to create healthy, balanced, free-flowing qi in our immediate surroundings.

Qi is produced by the on-going struggle between yin and yang (see page 22), and what feng shui aims to do is address any imbalances between them in your immediate environment, whether it's in your house or garden, to ensure you have the

WOOD

Its season: spring. Its shape: tall, rectangular. Green shades. Yin colour: light green. Yang colour: dark green. In the garden: upright woody plants and wooden structures.

The Five Elements relate to each other in two different cycles: one supporting, the other controlling. So Water supports Wood, which supports Fire, which supports Earth, which supports Metal, which in turn supports Water. In the other cycle, Water controls Fire, which controls Metal, which controls Wood, which controls Earth, which in turn controls Water.

To create an environment that is healthy and harmonious, you need to check out the balance of the elements, add any that are missing, beef up those that are too weak and tone down any that are too dominant. While it is comparatively easy to do this in a garden with some elements – earth or wood, for example – with others the balance can be redressed symbolically if not in reality. If, say, you need to add water to an area and a water feature isn't practical, you can add blue planting or, if it's fire that's missing, add an obelisk – triangles are a fire shape – or some red planting.

Over the centuries different schools of feng shui emerged. The original school is the Form or Landscape School, which looks exclusively at the garden and its environment. The second is the Compass School, which developed after the Chinese compass – the luo pan – was invented. This school takes into account a number of factors as well as readings with the luo pan itself, and looks not only at the garden but at the needs of the people who use it. You can use one school or the other, but they are undoubtedly more powerful when used together. While it is possible to apply

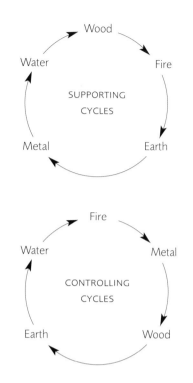

the Landscape form satisfactorily yourself, the Compass school requires considerable study or the services of an experienced feng shui consultant.

The Landscape School

The symbolic starting point for this school of feng shui is the 'four celestial animals', which determine the most auspicious location for a house. Since few of us have the luxury these days of choosing the most auspicious plot, the celestial animals can help you to make the most of what you've got. In this school of feng shui, the plot is treated as a whole, not as two separate spaces – front and back.

At the back of the house and garden to support and protect it should be the Black Turtle or Tortoise, originally the gentle slope of a hill, but these days it can be a building. If there is no hill or building there, you can plant trees or shrubs – but they must be on your land. Trees at the bottom of the neighbour's garden won't do the trick because their qi doesn't belong to you.

The smooth, curving lines in this garden, both in the path and in the shape of the beds, aids the smooth flow of qi round the garden.

To the front of the house is the Red Phoenix, which represents the future and is, ideally, a low area with an open aspect enabling you to see clearly ahead. To the right as you face the house is the Green Dragon, again traditionally a small hill or these days far more likely a building or planting, but whatever it is, it should be slightly smaller than the Tortoise. This is the yang side of the garden, which represents organization and structure. To the left is the White Tiger, the yin side, which should be slightly smaller than the Green Dragon and represents creativity and intuition. As feng shui consultant Betty Talks puts it, it's as if the house is sitting in a comfortable armchair, very well supported at the back and well supported at the sides.

Traditionally, there should be moving water at the front of the house, a gently flowing stream or small river, because it is a very powerful source of qi. These days, with most of us living in towns and cities,

a road will serve because the movement along it is also a source of qi. Obviously, it shouldn't be a major trunk road with traffic hurtling past day and night because that would create sha qi – bad energy – which in this instance is so fast-moving that it can get out of control. Such a location is also bad for your health. As I said earlier, a lot of feng shui is common sense.

Another source of sha qi, to be avoided or deflected, is straight lines or sharp angles pointing at your house – known as 'poison arrows'. A road heading directly for your house – if you live at a T-junction for example – or the right-angled corner of a neighbouring building pointing directly at your house produces sha qi. If possible, avoid telegraph poles, lamp-posts or tall trees outside your doors and windows since they – and their shadows – are a potential source of sha qi.

It is also very important to sort out any sha qi before you start to maximize the good qi in your garden. If you can't avoid it, then you can block or deflect bad energy in a number of ways. Planting is good way of blocking it – a clump of bamboo for example between you and the corner of a neighbouring house – but the plants must be healthy. If they are diseased or dying, remove them immediately as they are then a source of bad energy themselves, and look awful, too. Common sense again. You can use wind chimes to slow down fast-moving qi, and some practitioners use a reflective surface like a mirror, though ideally it should be a convex mirror to turn the image upside-down.

Water is another means of defusing sha qi, ideally moving, but it can be still – in a birdbath for example – provided it is always fresh and clean. Stagnant water creates stagnant energy, another type of sha qi.

The most auspicious shape for a house is square or rectangular, so if you have an L- or U-shaped house, you need to fill in the 'missing space'. It doesn't have to be with building – a conservatory, for example – but can be done symbolically with a water feature to bring missing energy into the space, a mirror that appears to fill in the space with reflections, or a light. Houses with courtyards are thought to be auspicious, though, because by planting in them you can bring nature right into the heart of the house.

Ideally, your house should be sited in the centre of the plot with boundaries to protect but not overpower it, so a 10m-high (33ft) leylandii hedge is out. Boundaries should follow natural contours of the landscape but, with most us living in urban areas on regular-shaped plots, fences or walls are far more likely. Ideally they should be at least 2m (6ft) from the house, to give a sense of enclosure, not imprisonment.

Although most of us pay more attention to our back gardens than we do to the front, in feng shui the front is probably more important. The position of the front door is key. It is like the mouth of the house, through which qi can enter, so it should be clear and open. There should be no large plants blocking it, and, if there is a front hedge, you should be able to see over it. If it is too tall it will block the flow of qi.

Deciding which is the front and which is the back can be difficult. If your house is on a hill sloping downwards away from the back of the house, perhaps you should make the back door the principal entrance.

The doorway should be free of all clutter, too – no stacks of logs, family wellies or bikes – because clutter is a source of sha qi. You can have plants in containers either side of the door: the one on the right, the Green Dragon side, slightly larger than the one on the left, the White Tiger side, but the plants, ideally evergreen, must be healthy and well cared for, and any that are dead or dying should be removed immediately.

The path and drive, if you have them, should be curved or semi-circular for preference. If they are straight and pointing directly at the house they are potentially poison arrows. The sha qi can be deflected by softening the straight edges with planting. If possible, there should be a step up into the house since qi flows in an upward direction.

If the door is the mouth of the house, the windows are the eyes, and need to be kept clear too. There should be no trees planted directly in front of them, nor branches growing across them. Some practitioners believe that growing climbers up the house is a bad idea because it means the house cannot breathe easily. But if you do have climbers growing up the house and you want to keep them, make sure that they are trimmed neatly around the windows.

The design of the back garden should

Water is an excellent means of deflecting sha qi, especially when it is moving. This simple water feature made from a bamboo gutter is oriental in feel.

take balance as its theme – a balance between man-made and natural, hard and soft, hot and cold and so forth. Paths should ideally curve gently, and should go right round the garden to allow the smooth flow of qi throughout the space. There should be no dead ends. If you have a pot on a path or as a focal point, place it so that it stands out from the wall or fence – then the qi can flow smoothly round it. Paving, pergolas and other features should also be curved, although some practitioners maintain you can have straight lines as long as they don't create poison arrows for your own house or anyone else's.

Water is a powerful source of qi in the garden, ideally flowing rather than still. If it's not practical to have a stream, then have a fountain in a pond or even a bubble fountain on the patio. Fountains are a better bet than waterfalls or spouting wall masks because in fountains the water, and therefore the energy, is going upwards rather than downwards. Still water is fine as long as it's not stagnant, so either have a well-balanced, healthy wildlife pond or still water in a small container that you can change frequently.

As for planting, on the Green Dragon side of the garden, the yang side, go for big, robust chunky plants, with plenty of evergreens. Look for plants with bold rounded leaves such as *Fatsia japonica*, *Magnolia grandiflora*, *Bergenia* – all of which are evergreen – and plants with a strong upright habit, reaching as it were to the heavens. If you use spiky plants like cordylines or mahonias, don't place them near paths or seating areas because they can create poison arrows. Choose 'hot' yang colours, too – reds, oranges and yellows – and if you have ornaments, choose strong shapes.

On the yin side of the garden, the White Tiger side, go for more delicate, graceful, willowy plants – birch or coyote willow, for example – and lower-growing creeping plants such as thyme for a sunny spot, or bugle (*Ajuga reptans*), lamium or ground-covering hardy geraniums for a shadier position. Here the colours should be softer and lighter.

The Compass School

If you have read anything about feng shui you will have seen the pa kua, an octagonal symbol with one of the eight trigrams – sets of three black lines of varying lengths representing Heaven, Earth and Humanity – in each segment, and a point of the compass in each one. Each segment represents different things: the south-east, for example, represents wealth, while the south-west represents relationships and marriage – hence people talk about the relationship corner in their homes.

Although the symbol of the pa kua itself is ancient, this form using the trigrams is very recent. It was introduced in the USA in the mid-1980s in an attempt to try and simplify a very complicated subject. It is also what is known at the Late Heaven sequence, which deals with the effects humanity has had on the Earth, and is meant to be used inside the home only, not outside in the garden. For that, you need the Early Heaven sequence which deals with the relationship between Earth and Heaven.

Crucial to the Compass School is, not surprisingly, a compass – the special Chinese compass, the luo pan. This is a very complex device, a square of metal in the centre of which is a magnetic needle. Like a normal compass, it is divided into 360 degrees but, unlike a normal compass, true north isn't simply north. It is subdivided into '3 Mountains', and they can be subdivided again. Since the objective in feng shui is always to balance up and make the best of what's there, this gives the practitioner more opportunity to

This bench, made by sculptor Steve Geliot for the healing garden at Worthing Hospital in West Sussex, not only provides a place to sit among the planting, but adds a valuable scuptural element to the garden.

find solutions to particular problems.

Surrounding the compass needle are up to twenty-two different circular bands, all inscribed with a vast amount of information. It can tell, for example, from where the qi is entering the garden and whether that energy is yin or yang. Some practitioners also use it to find ley lines. The compasses can be bought off the peg as it were, but most practitioners buy them from a feng shui master who commissions them specially.

As well as the luo pan, the Compass School also makes use of the lo shu square. This is an ancient, 'magic' numerological device divided into nine squares each with a number allocated. The classic form has five at the centre, and when you take three neighbouring squares together, whether vertically, horizontally or diagonally, the numbers always add up to 15. The numbers allocated to each square are not always the same, though, but the pattern of their relationship with each other remains unchanged.

This grid is then laid over a rough plan of the whole plot with the middle square of the top row aligned with south, and the middle square of the bottom row aligned with north – the reverse of the way compass points are used on plans in the West. The eight squares around the outside relate to the main compass points, and they give you information about the elements in your garden – for example, the element in the south-east corner is always Metal.

The next piece of information comes from the compass reading. East for instance is always three. The number relates again to an element. Next the numbers are allocated to each square according to the Fate period we are in. According to the Yuen Hom School, we are in the Period of eight Fates (other schools say it is seven or nine), so with that number in the centre of the lo shu, the number in the south-east corner is nine and the element that number relates to is Metal again.

So you could wind up for example with an area of the garden which is all Metal,

It is no wonder that gazing up into the fresh green canopy of a large tree is good for you in mind, body and spirit.

with nothing to support it, so since Earth supports Metal you need to add Earth. If you wind up with two Metal and one Wood, again the area lacks balance since Metal controls Wood, which has nothing to support it. The simple way to resolve the problem would be to add a middle-man, in this case Water, either the real thing or symbolically with dark blue planting, since Water supports Wood and so brings it into balance with Metal.

Before you do that, though, you need to take into account the final factor in the Compass School of feng shui – the horoscopes of the people who are going to use the garden, done not using the zodiac but according to the Five Elements. This means that if you take on a garden that has already been subjected to feng shui, it will need to be done again and adjusted to take account of your family members and their particular needs. The Landscape factors will still apply, but one crucial element in the Compass School won't.

Each square relates to a member of the family. For example, the south is the father, or man; the north, the mother or woman; the south-west, the eldest daughter; and the north-west, the youngest son. The

central square is for everyone. You apply the horoscope only to areas for which you have corresponding family members, and you balance the others in the way described above.

The horoscope is based on date, time and place of birth – each of which relates to an element revealed by consulting detailed Chinese charts. If you are all Water, say, you need Metal to support the Water, which may already be in your area of the garden from the lo shu reading. If not, add it either in reality or symbolically as white, gold, silver or bronze planting.

Perhaps you are Earth and so would need Fire to support you. Again, you may find Fire is already there from the lo shu reading but, if not, you can add it easily enough either as red or orange planting, or as a triangular shape such as an obelisk.

If your plot is an unusual shape, you may find that when you apply the lo shu to it there are missing spaces. The garden of feng shui consultant Betty Talks, for example, was made up of two squares, joined by a short path at one corner so that when the luo shu was applied, the north (the mother or woman) and the south (the father or man) were both missing. The simplest solution in that case was to put a gate between the two parts of the garden, creating two completely separate squares to which the luo shu could be applied individually. If that isn't possible, another solution is to strengthen the boundaries with the missing spaces in some suitable way – with yang planting and features for the south, and yin planting and features for the north.

JAPANESE GARDENS

Shinto, the earliest indigenous Japanese religion, has much in common with the Tao. It too believed in the Oneness of everything – physical and spiritual – and was also deeply rooted in nature. It revered mountains, rocks, water and trees, believing not so much that they contained spirits – kani – but that they offered access to them. So Shinto shrines were and still are gardens, often built around an old tree, with shrubs, meandering pathways, stone lanterns, often protected from outside by screens of plant material such as bamboo, wicker or even thatch, while the temple itself was always wood. Worship was silent contemplation.

By the time Buddhism reached Japan from China via Korea in the sixth century AD it had already merged with Taoism, and the form known in China as Chan but in the West as Zen Buddhism had emerged. Its founder, an Indian monk called Bodhidharma, believed that other forms of Buddhism had missed the essen-

tial point – that at the core of everything, there is nothing. The aim of a Buddhist monk was to meditate until his mind was clear of thought, his spirit freed and he could achieve the desired state of nothingness in which he would discover his true self. Zen gardens were designed to help him achieve his goal.

Unlike western gardens, which are designed to stimulate the senses, to change and grow, Zen gardens are designed to soothe, and remain the same.

While there several types of Zen garden, the best known are the dry gardens – kare-sensui – in which a whole world is suggested by rock, raked sand and just a few plants. Unlike Tao gardens in which we are an important active element, Zen gardens are designed purely to be seen, usually from inside a building. Having visited several, in Kyoto and in this country, I

Looking at this group of grasses, illuminated by the morning sun and partly shrouded in mist from the stream, it is easy to understand why ancient religions like Shinto saw plants and water as gateways to the spirits.

must say that they do have the most extra-ordinary effect on you. They calm you down almost immediately, slowing your thoughts, even your breathing, and the more you look at what appears to be very little, the more you see. The patterns of algae or moss on the rocks, the relationship between the groups of rocks, the way the light falls on the ridges in the sand …

These gardens are rich in symbolism. The rocks can represent a number of different things. In themselves they are revered as a legacy of the Shinto tradition, particularly if they are worn and weathered, and their great ages, often millions of years, are symbols of the impermanence of life. They can represent Heaven, a vertical rock, Earth, a horizontal one, and Human-ity, a diagonal linking the two. Three is an auspicious number, as are five and seven. At Roan-ji, one of the most famous of all Zen gardens, the rocks are grouped into three, five and seven. The rocks can repre-sent the Mystic Islands of the Blest where the Immortals dwell in great luxury, or a number of myths about dragons, cranes or the tiger and its cubs.

As with Taoist gardens, space is as important as the rocks themselves and the art of placing rocks was highly developed. Water is essential too, either the real thing or, as in dry gardens, represented by sand – though here too there is always a tsukobai, a stone basin full of water at the entrance to the garden for washing the hands and face and purifying the soul.

The sand is raked into different patterns – straight lines, or curves to represent the water lapping round the islands (the rocks) either gently or more wildly. The act of raking, like every task in the garden, is per-formed with love, and is part of the act of meditation.

Plants, too, where they are used are symbolic. The pine for instance, one of the Trees of Life along with the peach and the plum, is revered for its longevity and the fact that, although it is shaped by the elements, it is never broken by them, mak-ing it a symbol of triumph over adversity. Red-flowered camellias, which drop their flowers in full bloom, are seen to represent the power of death over humanity even in the prime of life.

In other types of Zen garden, where plants are much more prominent, they are used to mimic nature. Trees are artfully trained and pruned to represent the true essence of that particular tree, small-leafed azaleas are clipped to mimic the surround-ing landscape. Green is the predominant colour from the foliage and the moss, which is a feature of so many Zen gardens. What other colour there is in these gardens is restrained and ephemeral – blossom in spring, for example – to symbolize the fleeting nature of life.

Symbolic camellias.

THE HEALING GARDEN FOR THE MIND AND SPIRIT

Given the small size of the space we were working with, it just wasn't practical to screen off an area for contemplation from the rest of the garden, so we marked the division in different ways. To reach it, you have to cross water, a narrow rill, by means of stepping stones made with large, iridescent bubble marbles (see page 151). These are actually above the level of the water but they don't look as though they are, so you have to concentrate on what you are doing when you cross from the active, busy area of the garden into the quiet, reflective area.

Ideally the quiet contemplative area should involve a journey, an action that takes one away from everyday life. Again, in a small garden it's not easy to create this, which is why we decided on a spiral path. This is, if you like, a very simple form of

Left: A modern American take on the Japanese garden, with wood, rock and gravel the dominant elements, along with a few organic-looking pots, and colour restricted to a little greenery and the fiery scarlet of the bouganvillea.

labyrinth or maze – a very potent symbol dating back to Neolithic times. It's a very powerful Christian symbol, too, with the early church introducing a labyrinth with eleven rings to represent the eleven true apostles. It was symbolic of the soul's journey from darkness into the light. It can also be seen as a mandala, a symbolic diagram of the universe used in both Buddhism and Hinduism as an aid to

circle. The remaining curving section into the centre of the spiral was done freehand. The cobbles were laid on sand and the edges haunched with concrete to hold them firmly in place. The path is deliberately narrow, again to make you think about where you are walking, and so already helping you clear your mind of everyday thoughts.

We planted either side of the path with *Stipa tenuissima*, a delightful fine grass with fluffy seedheads, against which your legs

meditation into which you enter mentally and progress towards the centre.

We created a very simple form of spiral in our garden, so that as you walk into the centre, you are making a journey into yourself and then, as you walk out again, you wind yourself up ready to face the world again.

The path was built with small cobbles to give us the flexibility to make tight, smooth curves. We drew the shape with degradable marking spray, using a scaffolding board to mark the straight section in from the rill, and then a peg in the centre and string pulled tight to mark out a semi-

brush as you pass. The planting in the two raised beds was primarily restful greens with just a little white – ideal for contemplation, while the bamboo in each corner creates a gentle rustling sound as the wind passes through it, helping to mask the distracting noises of the world outside, as does the gentle gurgling noise from the water feature.

Arriving at the end of your 'journey', you would need something to sit on, so at the centre of the spiral we placed a canvas chair, light and easily moved so you could choose which direction you wanted to face.

Some people find it helpful in meditation to have an object to focus on. For something upon which to meditate, in the raised bed at the end of the rill we placed a simple round terracotta ball, and at the other end two beautiful, smooth, small white boulders.

Remarkably quickly, this area took on a different atmosphere from the rest of the garden, and made a space that really did make you want to slow down and chill out – the object of the exercise, after all.

YOUR GARDEN FOR THE MIND AND SPIRIT

As we have shown in the healing garden, it is not difficult to create an area for quiet contemplation within your garden. It doesn't have to be a large area, but ideally it should be reasonably private, somewhere you can sit and not be disturbed or overlooked, somewhere you feel enclosed and safe. Dappled shade is probably the ideal site, since full sun will be too hot on summer days and full shade too dank and depressing on overcast days. If there is no privacy, you will need to think about screening of some sort – a hedge perhaps, either a formal one of yew or some other conifer, or even better still an informal one, with attractive evergreen shrubs such

The spiral path in the contemplative area of the healing garden.

as *Choisya ternata*, *Hebe* or *Escallonia*.

Perhaps the quickest way is to build some kind of arbour or seating area, with a simple overhead structure over which you can grow climbing plants. Even before the plants have grown up that far, having structure over your head does create a strong sense of enclosure. Scented plants might be a good choice: honeysuckle, roses or jasmine, though if you think you might want to use it on bright winter days, then something evergreen might be worth having, too – white-flowered, scented *Clematis armandii* perhaps or, in a sheltered garden, star jasmine (*Trachelospermum jasminoides*).

It also needs to be quiet or, if that's not possible – and it might well not be in this increasingly noisy world – make sure you have natural sounds to mask at least some of the noises of modern life. According to a study carried out at a Canadian university, the noises to which primitive people were exposed were 70 per cent nat-

ural sounds, 25 per cent human voices and 5 per cent primitive tools. By 1973 natural sounds accounted for less than 6 per cent, the percentage for the human voice stayed the same and all the rest was machinery of different kinds. By now, the percentage of natural sounds must be even smaller.

Plants such as bamboo or aspen, whose leaves rustle in the breeze, are good choices. So is water. A gentle gurgling water feature, either in a pond or on a wall, is surprisingly effective in masking intrusive sounds from outside and in focusing your mind within the garden. Even if you live high up in a tower block with only a balcony, it is surprising how effective a small ceramic wall fountain can be in disguising the roar of the traffic below. Although not a natural sound, wind chimes – provided they are mellow and harmonious – can do a similar job.

Water is a marvellous element to include in any contemplative area for its visual properties, too. Still water, even in a

A Japanese-style corner in a suburban garden, with rocks, gravel, an architectural plant (*Phormium*), as well as a simple water feature.

small stone or metal basin, offers reflections of the sky, and if its interior is dark, the possibility of infinite depths (see page 148).

The 'journey' referred to earlier doesn't have to be far. All it needs to do is reinforce in your mind the idea that you are deliberately removing yourself from your everyday life. After a while, you will find that whenever you set off, your mind will start to clear and your heart rate and breathing will already be slowing down in anticipation.

And once you arrive at your destination, you need something to sit on. Since you will be spending some time there, the seat should be comfortable, but not so comfortable that you nod off. You'll be tempted to use it more often if it's left in position permanently, but if that's not feasible, make sure the seat is light and easy to move around, like the canvas chair used in the healing garden.

The area should be simple in its layout and in its planting. Rather than lots of different types of plants, it's much better to stick to a few. The contemplative garden designed by Dan Pearson for Worthing Hospital in West Sussex is a case in point. The main planting is *Stipa arundinacea*, a beautiful evergreen grass, which has delicate weeping seedheads in summer and a coppery tone to the leaves in winter. It responds to the slightest breeze, and the gentle movement brings life into the garden. As for the other planting, there is *Sedum* 'Autumn Joy', red-hot pokers (*Kniphofia*) and *Verbena bonariensis*, along with multi-stemmed silver birches (*Betula jacquemontii*) and the evergreen strawberry tree (*Arbutus unedo*). The bold waves of planting – eminently suitable for a seaside location – are very relaxing, because your eye happily rests on them and is not tempted to dart about.

The dominant colour in this garden is green, ideal as it is such a restful colour. Violet, too, the colour of the *Verbena bonariensis*, is a spiritual colour, also good for contemplation. (See Chapter 3 on colour for suitable plants.) There are enough splashes of seasonal colour to add a little spark, and in winter, when the leaves are off the silver birches, you have the beauty of white stems to gaze at.

If you like to have an object upon which to meditate, it could the bark of a beautiful tree, like the silver birch, or some other plant, or an object – a statue perhaps of the Buddha, or an Easter Island head, or piece of abstract sculpture. In Dan Pearson's garden at Worthing Hospital, which incidentally is filled with exciting art inside as well, there is a beautiful smooth stone sculpture by Peter Randall-Page. This is reminiscent of an old-fashioned bee skep crossed with a seashell and you could happily gaze at it for ages. To maintain the marine theme, there are benches with wavy backs, made by sculptor Steve Geliot, which are surprisingly comfortable to sit on, and also beautiful to look at when they are unoccupied.

Your object for contemplation might be something that has special significance for you – a piece of pottery made by a friend, perhaps, or a shell you brought back from a memorable trip, or, as in Zen gardens, a piece of natural rock. In this case, it is more important that the object is meaningful to you than that it fits in with the overall style of your garden. Place it where it stands out clearly from its surroundings – you don't want your eyes and brain to be struggling to delineate its outline when the objective is to slow down your thought processes.

By carefully considering all these elements – of space and light, sight and sound, water and planting – you should be able to create for yourself a haven for contemplation within your own garden.

Peter Randall-Page's sculpture is perfect for quiet contemplation.

Herbs for health

Since the very earliest times, we have used herbs not only for food but also for healing. Every great civilization of the past – Egyptian, Greek, Roman, Mayan – used plants, sometimes in very sophisticated ways, to heal wounds, cure disease, deaden pain, lift the spirits and balance the mind. In so-called primitive cultures in every part of the world, where no written or pictorial records exist, we know that plants have been used for healing for thousands of years. In many of those cultures – and in China and India – the traditions of herbal medicine remain unbroken and plants and techniques used five thousand years ago are still in use today.

Anethum graveolens (Dill)

In the West, the industrial and scientific revolution in the eighteenth and nineteenth centuries led to the development of synthetic drugs, and herbal medicine largely fell by the wayside, dismissed as primitive, superstitious and – worse – unscientific.

It was only in the latter part of the twentieth century, with people becoming increasingly concerned about the side-effects accompanying the undoubted benefits of some drugs, that interest in natural remedies revived.

These days, every bright young thing seems to be taking echinacea drops to ward off colds and flu by boosting the immune system, and St John's wort is being hailed as nature's Prozac – and with good reason. A study published in the *British Medical Journal* in August 2000 showed it to be as effective in cases of mild depression as conventional anti-depressant drugs, and with fewer side-effects.

Herbs are undoubtedly back in favour in every way. After years when curly parsley (to garnish anything and everything), rosemary (for the lamb) and mint (for the new potatoes), were about the only herbs you saw in any kitchen, we now use a wide range of them in our cooking all the time. Herb teas are sold alongside the regular kind in every supermarket, and a whole range of toiletries and household products proclaim their wholesomeness to the world with the word 'herbal' on the label.

We now grow many herbs in our gardens or window-boxes, not only for their usefulness but also for their beauty. *Rosmarinus* 'Miss Jessopp's Upright' is an invaluable small-scale architectural evergreen, while smoky purple sage is a perfect underplanting for pink roses, and bronze fennel woven through a border is a wonderful foil for hot, tropical-looking cannas or *Crocosmia* 'Lucifer'.

HERBS IN HISTORY

Herbs are a group of plants defined by the *Oxford Dictionary* first of all as those whose stems do not become woody and which die down to the ground after flowering – hence 'herbaceous' – and secondly as 'plants of which the leaves or stem and leaves are used for food or medicine, or for their scent or flavour'. The Emperor Charlemagne gave his own definition in the eighth century AD. When asked by the monk Alcuis what a herb was he is said to have replied, 'A friend of physicians and the praise of cooks.'

The first recorded use of the word 'herb' in English was by the fourteenth-century radical priest John Wyclif, who wrote about 'erbis of vertue that growen', but the first evidence of the use of herbs goes back a great deal further – some 60,000 years earlier. In 1963 archaeologists in Iraq excavating a cave uncovered the grave of a man whose remains, dating techniques revealed, were 60,000 years old. Lots of plants had obviously been buried with him because there were many pollen grains in the grave. Analysis revealed that among them were pollen grains of hollyhock (*Althaea*) a soothing remedy for inflammation, yarrow (*Achillea*) an astringent and antiseptic, horsetail (*Equisetum*) a remedy for consumption and dysentery, and ephedra, an antispasmodic and stimulant, from which western medicine has extracted ephidrene, a valuable decongestant for asthma, hay fever and similar conditions.

There is of course no way of knowing how or why herbs were used at a time long before written records. While it is likely that flowers were in the grave for much the same reason as we send flowers to funerals today, it's also likely that they were there for their healing and symbolic properties as well.

The first hard evidence of how herbs were used in healing comes much later,

though still five thousand years ago in Egypt in the reign of Zoser, a pharaoh of the Third Dynasty a little after 3000 BC. We know from records that his physician was Imhotep, who was also his chief adviser, an astrologer, magician and architect of pyramids into the bargain. After Zoser's death, his palace became a temple of healing and eventually Imhotep himself was raised to the status of a god, with temples built in his honour in Memphis and Thebes. Statues of him survive, usually showing him reading a papyrus scroll.

Another papyrus, the Ebers papyrus, which was written around 2000 BC and acquired by the German Egyptologist Georg Ebers in 1873, lists medical conditions, ranging from crocodile bite to painful toenails, and the medicines used to treat them. Eighty-five herbs are listed from senna and castor oil to dill, mint, lettuce and poppy, and recipes given. The suggested cure for diarrhoea, for instance, includes figs, grapes, bread dough, fresh earth, onion and elderberries. And of course herbs played a large part in the preservation of bodies by mummification.

Herbs were also a vital element in religious ceremonies, not only in Egypt but in all early civilizations, and healers were usually priests too. In Babylon, now Iraq, the two functions were largely split. The 'ashipu' was a priest treating patients by intervening on their behalf with the gods, who were considered responsible in part for some illnesses, while the 'asu' was a

The medicinal herb garden at Southampton University is beautiful as well as useful

healer who worked with herbal medicines and even undertook surgery.

Surviving stone tablets record information in cuneiform about the herbs used for healing. These include liquorice, mint, sesame oil (which was applied to wounds after surgery as an antibiotic) and henbane (*Hyoscyamus niger*), a potent remedy for relieving pain and inducing sleep. It's so potent in fact that it is poisonous in every part – it may have been the poison that killed Hamlet's father, and a compound extracted from the plant is what Dr Crippen used to murder his wife.

CHINA

In China, although the approach to the whole subject of diagnosis and healing was different, with qi, yin and yang and the Five Elements (see pages 24–5) all playing their part, herbal remedies were important from the earliest time. In the *Pen Ts'ao* by Shen Nang (sometimes Shen Ziang), dating from the third millennium BC, 366 plants used medicinally at the time are listed, including ephedra, known by its Chinese name of mahuang. The *Nei Ching*, or *Yellow Emperor's Canon of Internal Medicine*, the definitive version of which dates from 200 BC (although some of it is thought to have been written much earlier, during the Yellow Emperor's reign), formed the basis of Chinese medicine as it is still practised today – not only in the East but also increasingly in the West. Many high streets now boast a Chinese herbalist as well as a pharmacy, and western complementary practitioners often include Chinese herbal remedies in their repertoire.

INDIA

Ayurveda, which means knowledge or science (*veda*) of life (*ayur*) in Sanskrit, is a system of thought embracing religion, philosophy and science as well as medicine. Since it is largely an oral tradition, there is little documentary evidence as to when it started, but it is thought to have developed between 5000 and 3000 BC among the Rishi, a group of spiritually enlightened beings who lived in a very remote area in the Himalayas. The key texts, *Caralea Samhitu* and *Susruta Samhita*, dating from between 200 BC and AD 200, list some 700 healing plants. Like Chinese medicine, its principles have hardly changed over thousands of years, and it is still practised in much the same way today.

It sees energy and matter as one and the same. It makes no distinction between the external and internal, and believes that human beings are a microcosm of the cosmos. Like Chinese medicine it believes in the Five Elements – ether or space, air, fire, water and earth, which relate to various parts of the body and to the five senses. From these come the three basic forces, the doshas, which control our physical, mental and spiritual state. Vata, the air principle, comes from ether and air; pitta, the fire principle, comes from fire and water; while kapha comes from earth and water.

As with so many complementary therapies, the objective in healing is always balance. If the doshas are balanced, we are healthy in mind, body and spirit. If they are not, we are not. In addition, there has to be the right balance between our prakruti – our basic constitution, the balance of dosha with which we are born – and our vkruti, the one that we have created for ourselves through the way we live. Once the Ayurvedic healer has diagnosed the imbalance, medicine is prescribed to correct it, as well as advice on changing lifestyle where necessary. Some medicines are mineral, but most are herbal and though the names seem unfamiliar– yavani, for example, kum-kuma, ahiphenam, jeeratra – many of the herbs are not. They are henbane, saffron, poppy and cumin respectively.

GREECE

Herbs for healing were an important part of Greek culture from the earliest times, and crop up in many of the myths. Asclepius, son of Apollo the sun god, was the healer, and his symbol, the serpent, is still a

Golden hop (*Humulus lupulus aureus*).

widely used symbol of medicine today. Healing was a gift of the gods, and illness a punishment from them, so the role of the priest-healer was to intervene on behalf of the patient with prayer and rituals involving herbs, which were also given to the patient.

Hippocrates (468–377 BC) was the first to approach healing on a scientific basis, seeing disease as having natural, as opposed to supernatural, causes, and proposing cures that were rational, as opposed to largely irrational. Along with herbal remedies – he recorded the use of some 400 medicinal plants – he also prescribed fresh air, exercise and a good diet, which remain excellent advice two and a half thousand years on. Hippocrates believed in the Five Elements – ether, air, fire, water, earth, the same five as Ayurvedic rather than Chinese medicine – and the four 'humours' (or human characteris-

tics) that arose from them: sanguine from air, choleric from fire, phlegmatic from water, and melancholic from earth. The balance between them all determined not only personality but body type, and an imbalance led to illness. The role of the healer was to diagnose the imbalance and treat it accordingly. So an excess of fire, for example, called for a remedy that cooled and moistened like lettuce or dandelion.

In 331 BC Alexander the Great founded a centre of learning at Alexandria in Egypt, where all the knowledge of the Egyptian, Sumarian and Assyrian healing traditions was brought together with the Greek. Over the next few hundred years Greek healers built on Hippocrates' work. Theophrastus wrote the *Enquiry into Plants* listing 500 medicinal herbs such as rose, myrtle, coriander and bay. Galen, who studied at Alexandria, worked as doctor to the gladiators in Greece and went to Rome in AD 162

Mediaeval apothecaries collecting plants to make into remedies. This is from a Latin manuscript, *The Art of the Apothecary*, held in the Eton College library.

Comfrey (*Symphytum officinale*), sometimes called knitbone, is an ancient remedy for healing all manner of wounds.

as doctor to the emperor Marcus Aurelius. He produced *De Simplicibus*, which combined the knowledge of all the great healing traditions as well as discoveries of his own, such as the fact that blood moved, and the value of taking a pulse.

It was Dioscorides, another Greek working as a doctor with the Roman army and travelling widely through what was known as Asia Minor in the second century AD, who wrote the definitive work. *De Materia Medica* collated all the information about healing known at the time, including 500 medicinal plants such as marjoram, fennel, garlic, basil, mint, rue, hellebore, belladonna and calamine. It was meticulously illustrated with plants drawn from life, and it became the foundation of European medicine for the next thousand years and more.

HEALING IN EUROPE

As the Romans conquered much of Europe and Asia Minor, they took their – or rather the Greeks' – medical knowledge with them. With the rise of Christianity, though, things started to change. The church believed that it should have exclusive control over healing, and so anything that smacked of the pagan or the infidel was suppressed in Christendom during the

Dark Ages and virtually all scientific research came to a halt.

Fortunately, the 'infidels' in their great centres of learning in Baghdad, Cairo and Damascus preserved the Greek medical knowledge and developed it along with their own. By AD 900 all surviving medical texts had been translated into Arabic. Like the Roman armies before them, the Arab invaders of Spain in the sixth and seventh centuries took their healing knowledge with them.

It wasn't until the eleventh century, though, when the Arabic texts – both original work and their translations of the Greek – were translated into Latin in France and Italy, and famous medical schools such as those at Salerno and Montpellier were established, that the knowledge of healing plants spread through Europe again. Or perhaps one should say 'official' knowledge, because the use of herbs for healing in so-called folk remedies had continued throughout this time. In Britain there was a strong Anglo-Saxon culture of healing. Most communities had their 'wise woman' who would seek to cure all ills with herbal potions, and sometimes with incantations and charms, too. *Wicca*, the Old English word for such a wise woman, came to mean witch, and of course many of the women who were later persecuted as witches were simply healers. The link between the two has taken a long time to die out. When Anne MacIntyre set up in practice as a medical herbalist in rural Gloucestershire twenty years ago, a neighbour asked her if she was responsible for the magpies he had found hanging in the woods, while a child asked her in all seriousness to turn another troublesome child into a frog!

In about 950 Bald, a monk alleged to have been close to King Alfred, asked a scribe called Cild to write down all the existing information about healing plants

Herbs grow well in pots and are not only useful but also decorative.

renewed interest in herbals and many beautiful illustrated books were made. The development of printing meant that books could be made far more quickly and cheaply, and therefore the information could be disseminated more easily.

The next major development in herbal medicine came in the early sixteenth century with the Swiss-German physician Paracelsus (real name Theophrastus Bombastus von Hohenheim) and the Doctrine of Signatures. According to this, the appearance of the plant signifies its healing potential – a gift from God to help humanity locate the plants it needed. So as the spotted leaves of lungwort (*Pulmonaria*) resembled the lungs, it must be a good cure for lung conditions – hence its common name. Interestingly, its botanical name comes from the Latin word for lung, in the same way that *Hepatica*, thought to resemble the liver and therefore be a cure for liver problems, comes from the Greek word for liver.

Plants such as dock that produce yellow sap, which resembles yellow bile, were also thought to be good for the liver. In fact it turns out that the latter is true, but in general terms the Doctrine of Signatures turned out to have little merit. An arrogant man whose chosen name means 'Beyond Celsus' (Celsus was a great first-century Roman doctor), Paracelsus publicly burned the books of Hippocrates, Galen and Avicenna as heretical in 1527. His lasting legacy was to introduce chemicals such as mercury and sulphur into medical treatment, thus uniting chemistry and medicine for the first time.

being used in the traditional ways. One of the few surviving herbals not to have been based on Greek or Arabic knowledge, it was called the *Leech Book of Bald*. It contains plants such as yarrow (*Achillea*), lungwort (*Pulmonaria*), wood betony (*Stachys betonica*) and vervain (*Verbena officinalis*). Incidentally, the word 'officinalis' or 'officinale' in the plant's botanical name means that it was used for healing.

During the Dark Ages, the church had taken responsibility for healing. In monasteries, monks translated and copied existing manuscripts, and shared knowledge with other monasteries throughout Europe, but no further research was done. Herb gardens were established in monasteries early on, located next to the infirmary. With the Renaissance came a

English herbals

Back in England, the sixteenth and early seventeenth centuries were the golden age of herbals. There was William Turner's *A New Herball* (1551), important because it was the first to be written in English, not

Latin, and so available to people other than physicians. John Gerard's *The Herball or Generall Historie of Plantes*, to give it its full title, is better known and still quoted today. He also grew what he wrote about, and it is said that in his garden at Holborn there were over a thousand different plants. John Parkinson, apothecary to James I, also had a garden in what is now central London, this time in Long Acre, Covent Garden. He wrote two books, *Paradisii in Sole Paradisius Terrestris* ('Park in Sun's Earthly Paradise' – a pun on his own name) and *Theatrum Botanicum*, in which he lists over 3800 plants.

Perhaps the most famous herbalist of the period was Nicholas Culpeper, whose *Herball* is still in print and whose name lives on in a chain of British shops selling a range of herbal products, from body lotion to tea. Astrology was one of his guiding principles, both in diagnosing symptoms and in categorizing the herbs to cure them. Marigold, for instance, was 'a herb of the sun and under Leo they strengthen the heart exceedingly'. The recipe he gave was a paste of dried flowers mixed with 'hog's grease' – lard, presumably – turpentine and rosin applied to the breast.

He was a controversial figure, angering the College of Physicians by translating their bible, the *Pharmacopoeia*, from Latin into English so that lay people could read it, and also by treating the poor for free. Some people feel his contribution to herbal medicine was a mixed blessing, in that his reliance on astrology laid it open to attack by the rationalists who came later.

Physic gardens

Although the monasteries had had medicinal herb gardens for centuries, it wasn't until the sixteenth century that the first secular 'physick' gardens were established. They had two purposes: first, to provide apothecaries with the raw materials for herbal medicines, and secondly, to teach students about the plants. The first was at

A chamomile seat is a wonderfully relaxing place to sit and a more practical option for most busy gardeners than a chamomile lawn.

Pisa in 1543. Other gardens in Germany, France and Holland followed. The Clusius Garden at Leiden in Holland, now a part of the Botanic Garden, has been meticulously restored to its original state. The first in England was founded by Oxford University in 1621. It was called the Oxford Physic Garden until 1840, when it became the Oxford Botanic Garden, reflecting the fact that botany – the study of plants in their own right – was now a proper scientific discipline, and considered far more important than medical botany.

The Chelsea Physic Garden in London, the only one to retain its original name, was founded in 1673 by the Society of Apothecaries for the training of apprentices who used to travel down the Thames by barge from the City. This was possible because until the Embankment was built in the 1870s the garden ran right down to the river's edge. Like all physic gardens, it was walled for protection from the elements – and from vandals and thieves, since some of the plants were rare and therefore valuable, especially from the late sixteenth century on when plant collectors began bringing back all sorts of treasures from abroad.

The gardens were laid out formally and the plants grouped in beds. There are no records to show how they were grouped originally, whether it was according to the area of the body they treated – skin, digestion, nervous system and so on – or to the healing characteristics of the plants – astringent, antiseptic, diuretic – but an engraving of 1751 shows the medical plants laid out alphabetically. Today the Chelsea Physic Garden still has a medicinal walk, displaying the history of healing plants from Dioscorides onwards, a garden of world medicine, showing medicinal plants from different cultures, and a bed planted with all the major drug plants in legitimate use today.

THE ADVENT OF SCIENCE

While new plants were being collected from all over the world, and brought back to England, attitudes were beginning to change. In the eighteenth century, the Age of Enlightenment brought a rational, scientific approach to everything. Man was no longer part of nature but separate from – even superior to – it, able to tame and exploit it for his own needs. Mind and body were also considered as separate, and the whole idea of holistic medicine, treating the whole person rather than a collection of symptoms, began to disappear. Doctors began prescribing metals such as mercury and chemicals such as arsenic rather than plants. In the formal gardens of the time herbs had no place except along with vegetables in the kitchen garden. They survived in cottage gardens, of course, and herbal medicines were still used among the poor who could not afford to pay doctors' bills.

In the nineteenth century the advance of science continued. Plants were still used, but were screened for their active chemical ingredients, which were synthesized and prescribed as drugs aimed at particular symptoms. This approach was the complete opposite of that taken by medical herbalists, who believe in the holistic approach – not only that you treat the person not the disease, but that the power to heal lies in the whole leaf or flower or root, not in one isolated chemical ingredient. Herbal medicine survived but was considered superstitious, cranky, fringe, alternative.

It wasn't really until the late 1960s and Flower Power that interest began to revive. There was a growing awareness of green issues with people seeing themselves once more as part of the natural world, not detached from or superior to it. Then there was the evolution of the Gaia theory in the late 1970s, a new world view that went

St John's wort (*Hypericum*) is an ancient remedy, the full extent of whose remarkable healing properties is still being discovered.

Left: The scented leafed pelargonium (*P.* 'Graveolens') makes a striking standard in a pot.

further and saw the Earth and all plant and animal life as one giant organism with the power to regulate, adapt, protect and heal itself. The Gaia theory was evolved by British atmospheric chemist James Lovelock, whose reputation as a scientist was such that he was asked by NASA to develop equipment for analysing the atmosphere on Mars to see whether life was sustainable. Lovelock freely admitted that the basic idea was not entirely new. It has its roots in medieval notions about human beings as microcosms of the macrocosm, in Renaissance ideas that people and planets worked in conjunction, in Culpeper's astrological herbalism, and in the work of Scottish geologist Dr James Hutton, who in 1785 claimed that the Earth is a superorganism and that the circulation of water on the planet, for example, could be compared to the circulation of blood in the human body.

There was also growing concern from the 1960s on about the side-effects of many powerful drugs – and more recently about the fact that many diseases thought to have been conquered have developed strains resistant to them. While it would be foolish to suggest that all drugs are bad – many have saved literally millions of lives – it would be equally foolish to dismiss thousands of years of knowledge and experience of herbal medicine from all over the world, and ignore the pharmacy you have growing in your garden.

HOW HERBAL MEDICINE WORKS

Herbal medicine works in a number of ways. It can be a useful preventive, boosting the body's immune, hormone and nervous systems, helping to prevent the onset of disease and, if it does take a hold, enabling you to recover from it more

Many relatives of the common or garden sage, such as *Salvia leucantha*, are beautiful, but do not have such potent healing properties.

quickly. It is a complementary treatment, and can work alongside conventional medical treatments, although if you are already taking prescription drugs, always consult a practitioner before you take herbal remedies. The enzymes in the liver, which metabolize some common herbal remedies, are those that also metabolize a large number of drugs. If you are taking both, then the enzymes involved in metabolizing the herbal remedy aren't available to break down the drugs, giving you in effect an overdose of the latter. While St John's wort (*Hypericum perforatum*) has been proved to be a useful antidepressant, there can be a harmful reaction if it is taken with prescription drugs such as the blood-thinning drug Warfarin or the antibiotic tetracycline. Another recent study published in the medical journal *The Lancet* also shows it can cause the body to metabolize too quickly certain drugs used to treat Aids and prevent transplant rejection, and so reduce their effectiveness.

Herbal medicine is a holistic treatment. Medical herbalists not only ask patients about their symptoms but also about their lives so that they understand all the factors that have brought them to this point. If those factors are not addressed, then even if the symptoms are dealt with successfully there is every likelihood that they will recur. Medical herbalist and author Anne MacIntyre has a response to people who ask if she has a remedy for a headache –'No, but I have remedies for people'. This is not dissimilar to the old saying, 'Ask not what manner of disease the man has, but what manner of man has the disease.' Two people may have very similar symptoms, but these may well have resulted from totally different causes, and so the remedies prescribed will be very different too.

While it may seem that swallowing a capsule containing a herbal remedy and one of a prescription drug are more or less

the same, the fact is they work in very different ways. Drugs, even when they are synthesized from plants, extract one chemical element and are designed to treat a particular symptom. A herbal remedy uses the entire extract of the plant, whether it's from the leaves, flowers, berries, bark or roots, with all its chemical constituents – rue (*Ruta graveolens*) for example has 110 different compounds.

There is also the fact that the individual elements can act as a buffer to each other, preventing any unwanted side-effects. A prime example of this is meadowsweet (*Filipendula ulmaria*). It is a rich source of salicylic acid – the chemical name for aspirin – and so is a useful analgesic and anti-inflammatory. Unlike aspirin itself, which causes bleeding in the stomach and gut and associated digestive problems if taken long term, *Filipendula* contains compounds that are an excellent treatment for a range of stomach problems from acidity to ulcers.

Herbalists believe that the synergy between the different compounds contained in a plant is more effective even than the sum of all the individual parts. This is one reason why it has not been possible to run the sort of analytical chemical trials to which prescription drugs are subjected. A team of researchers at the University of Middlesex, which has run a BSc degree in herbal medicine for the last six years, is now looking for ways of testing the effectiveness of the whole plant as well as finding new remedies. In 2000 they embarked on a trial using sage as a treatment for Alzheimer's disease. It contains a substance that also occurs in the brain called acetylcholine, diminishing levels of which have been linked to memory loss. Perhaps it is no coincidence that 'sage' means wise.

It is possible to grow medicinal herbs in any back garden, either in special herb gardens or in mixed borders, as they are such attractive plants.

Many medicinal herbs, such as borage, have a number of different uses, both internal and external.

Leaves

With aromatic leaves, the best time to pick them is just before the plant flowers because their aromatic oils are at their most concentrated then. For the same reason, you should pick them in the morning when the sun has dried off any dew but before it is hot enough to vaporize the oils. Handle them carefully as you collect them so as not to bruise them.

Flowers

Flowers should be picked just after the buds have started to open, but are not yet in full flower. Pick them on a dry day.

Seeds

These should be harvested when they are fully ripe. The trick is to catch them before they drop or are scattered. Cut off the ripe seedhead carefully and place it upside-down in a paper bag, to catch the seeds as they drop. If the seeds are almost ripe but not quite, place a paper bag over the seed-head, gather it tightly underneath and tie it round the stem with string.

Berries

Collect these at the peak of their ripeness.

Bark

This should be stripped from a branch that has been pruned off the plant. Spring/early summer is the ideal time when the nutrients are at their most concentrated just underneath the bark.

Roots

These are best harvested just after the top growth has died down completely in autumn because they are then full of the nutrients intended to produce next year's foliage and flowers. You can also harvest them in spring before they start into growth again, but unless you've marked their location it's less easy to find them

A WORD OF WARNING

Herbal remedies are potentially very powerful and should be treated with great respect. Not everything that is natural is harmless – some plants are extremely, not to say fatally, poisonous. The standard culinary herbs are safe to ingest in the usual ways, but before you take anything else from the garden you should always ask the advice of a practitioner.

You should be cautious with herbal remedies bought over the counter, too. While in themselves they are safe, there can be problems in some instances if they are taken with prescription drugs (see page 50).

HOW TO PREPARE HERBAL REMEDIES

For most herbal remedies you can use fresh herbs when they are at their best, or you can dry them for use during the rest of the year. Some can be frozen.

then. Dig them up carefully to avoid damaging the root, wash off all the soil, and remove any traces of dead top growth. They will dry more quickly if you cut them into slices.

Drying herbs

If they are not being used fresh, they need to be dried quickly to preserve their potency. The key to success is to make sure they are thoroughly dry before you store them. If there is any moisture left in them, they will deteriorate fast.

Keeping the varieties separate, either hang them in bunches or spread them on a tray, or better still a wire cooling tray so that air can circulate all round them. Leave them in a warm, dry place – not a kitchen because there can be too much steam from pans and kettles and the temperature fluctuates. An even temperature of 27–32 degrees C (80–90 degrees F) is ideal, so the airing cupboard, over an Aga if you have one or in the bottom of the oven with the door left open, allowing air to circulate and moisture to evaporate, are all good options.

Once you are sure they are completely dry – and that can take between three and seven days – crumble leaves and flowers,

making sure you have removed all stems, break roots and bark into small pieces and store them ideally in dark glass jars. If you only have clear glass jars make sure the herbs are stored in the dark, since exposure to light will reduce their potency for healing. Label them clearly with the name of the herb and the date on which you stored them. Dried berries can be stored whole in glass jars, and seeds are best stored in paper packets or envelopes in an airtight container.

Dried herbs should keep their effectiveness for about a year – at least through the winter and spring until fresh herbs are available again.

DIFFERENT TYPES OF REMEDY

The method best suited to each herb will be listed in the plant's profile, starting on page 62. Some are taken internally, while others are applied externally.

To be taken internally

Many herbal remedies can be absorbed into the body via the digestive system.

TEAS, TISANES AND INFUSIONS

This is the easiest way of making a herbal remedy and the one that is most commonly used – peppermint tea after a meal to aid digestion, chamomile to calm you down and help you sleep. It couldn't be simpler. For one 300ml (half-pint) mug, place 25g (1oz) of fresh herbs or 15g ($^{1}/_{2}$oz – difficult to measure $12^{1}/_{2}$g!) of dried herbs in a jug, top up with water that is just off the boil and leave to infuse for 10 minutes. Then strain into the mug. You can make a larger quantity and store some in an airtight container in the fridge. While bought tea bags are fine as a drink, for medicinal purposes it's much better to use

Purple sage (*Salvia officinalis* 'Purpurascens') has the same healing properties as the plain green kind and is a wonderful foil for pinks and mauves in any border.

herbs you've grown yourself, because you'll know how they have been grown and how old they are.

You can use a mixture of herbs. Feverfew is good for headaches, but is bitter on its own, so add some peppermint or lemon balm to make it more palatable.

DECOCTIONS

These are similar to infusions except that you need to boil harder parts of the plant – bark, seeds, roots – to release their healing properties. First grind up the herbs in a pestle and mortar, or in an electric coffee grinder kept specially for the purpose. You'll need 50g (2oz) fresh herbs or 25g (1oz) of dried herbs and 650ml (just over a pint) of water. Place the herbs and the water in a stainless steel or enamel pan (not aluminium), bring up to the boil and then simmer, covered, for 10–15 minutes. Strain the liquid off and either drink it right away or store in the fridge.

Note that infusions and decoctions can also be used externally, in poultices, salves and so on (see below).

SYRUPS

You can make a syrup with either infusions or decoctions for adults and particularly children with a sweet tooth. You need 600ml (1 pint) of double-strength infusion or decoction, 325g (12oz) runny honey and 325g (12oz) unrefined brown sugar. Mix them all together in a stainless or enamel pan and bring slowly to the boil, skimming off the scum that forms on the surface. When the mixture has thickened slightly, leave it to cool, then pour into bottles and seal with a cork.

TINCTURES

These are made by soaking fresh herbs in alcohol and dried herbs in a mixture of water and alcohol. The advantage with tinctures is that you only need very small amounts. They are easy to use internally and externally and they last for up to two years. The precise recipe varies from herb to herb, since different herbs need different strengths of alcohol to extract their healing constituents – meadowsweet needs only 50 per cent alcohol, for example, while a tincture of calendula needs 70 per

Herbs grown in neat rows in a simple brick-edged potager at Hollington Herb Garden near Newbury.

cent – so you should consult a herbal pharmacopoeia.

You could use cider vinegar and raspberries to make raspberry vinegar, which is good for coughs and sore throats.

CAPSULES

While you can't make tablets at home, it's relatively easy to make your own herbal capsules. You can buy hollow gelatine capsules in different sizes from specialist suppliers, and you simply fill these with powdered herbs.

To be used externally

The active constituents of herbal remedies can also be absorbed through the skin and via the nasal passages – as in aromatherapy. In addition to essential oils (see page 117), you can add infusions or decoctions or tinctures to bathwater – in hand- and foot-baths as well as the regular kind – or to poultices, salves and so forth.

POULTICES

An ancient remedy, a poultice is made with either fresh or dried herbs worked into a paste by pounding in a pestle and mortar (using fresh), or mixing with water (using dried). Spread enough to cover the area to be treated between two pieces of muslin, and tie in place with a bandage.

COMPRESSES

Used either hot or cold, these can relieve swelling and bring down temperature. Soak a flannel or piece of towel in a cold or hand-hot infusion or decoction, wring it out well, and put on the affected area. Repeat often as the flannel gets either too warm or too cool.

CREAMS AND SALVES

You can make your own creams, by adding infusions, decoctions, tinctures or essential oils into a plain aqueous cream base that you can buy from the chemist. You could also make salves, by mixing your chosen herb into a bowl in which you have already melted 450ml (16fl oz) olive oil and 50g (2oz) beeswax. Heat it over a pan of simmering water for at least two hours, checking to make sure that the pan doesn't boil dry. When the mixture is cool enough to touch, pour it into a muslin jelly bag and squeeze the oil and wax through it into a glass storage jar, leaving the herbs behind. Leave it to solidify and store in a cool place.

In some instances, you can simply apply a leaf to the skin – a lemon balm (*Melissa*) leaf applied to a cold sore takes the swelling down with remarkable speed.

HEALING PLANTS IN THE HEALING GARDEN

Given that space is very limited in the healing garden, we decided to grow our healing plants in mixed beds as well as in a small, designated herb area. The herb bed was shaped like the stylized silhouette of a house between the junction of the paths from the gate and back door and the deck. This was an ideal spot – easily accessible from the kitchen in all weathers, and also from the deck, so if you wanted to pick a sprig of mint for your Pimms or throw some angelica seeds into the chimenea you could do so almost without leaving your chair.

To divide the space up, we used the same small cobbles as we had used to make our spiral path in the contemplative area (see page 34), and laid a couple of single rows, following the lines of the bed itself. To keep things simple, we just laid them directly on to compacted soil.

As a focal point, and a link to the rest of the garden, we placed a terracotta sphere in the centre at the deck end, and planted tall herbs – angelica, lovage and fennel –

Valerian (*Valeriana officinalis*) is a desirable garden plant for its looks alone. Its root provides a valuable remedy for a range of stress-related conditions.

beside it. The contrast between the smooth simple lines of the sphere and the jagged leaves of the angelica and lovage, and the fine feathery bronze leaves of the fennel, was an especially pleasing one. By the end of the summer, these tall herbs also created a screen at the back of the deck, adding a sense of enclosure.

We also planted purple sage, chamomile, marjoram, chives, rosemary and thyme. While you want to include as many different plants as possible, remember that you need quite large quantities of each herb if you are using them regularly.

In another small bed by the back door, we planted mint so that it could rampage to its heart's content. We also planted another lovage there too since this can

reach up to 2.5m (about 8ft) tall. Elsewhere in the garden, we grew prostrate rosemary to spill over the edges of the raised beds at either end of the rill, *Echinacea purpurea*, the dwarf lady's mantle (*Alchemilla erythropoda*) and a hedge of lavender (*L. angustifolia*) between the deck and the rill.

GROWING MEDICINAL HERBS AND OTHER PLANTS IN YOUR GARDEN

Whether you have a large garden, a small garden, a balcony, or even only a windowsill, you have room to grow some medicinal plants. Equally, whether it's sunny or shady, the soil is heavy or more like sand,

1 Thyme (golden)
2 Chives
3 Marjoram
4 Purple sage
5 Lemon thyme
6 Parsley
7 Roman chamomile
8 Angelica
9 Fennel
10 Lovage
11 Terracotta ball
12 Rosemary
13 Cobbles

you will still find some plants that will grow, if not in your borders, then in pots where you can give them the conditions they really like.

First of all, decide which plants you would like to grow, then look at your garden and see whether you have a suitable spot. In a sunny garden with free-draining soil, you can grow all of the Mediterranean herbs that are culinary as well as medicinal – rosemary, fennel, thyme, sage, coriander. If it's sunny, but the soil is damp and heavy, then you need to improve the drainage with plenty of grit and perhaps some leaf mould or soil conditioner with a little compost, which will open up the texture but won't add nutrients to the soil. Since these herbs don't enjoy too rich a soil, don't add only compost if you can avoid it. Mint, on the other hand, likes moist, even boggy soil, as do angelica, comfrey (*Symphytum officinale*) and meadowsweet (*Filipendula ulmaria*). If your soil is impossibly heavy, grow your Mediterranean herbs separately in gritty compost in pots.

While these herbs like full sun, many others, such as chives, fennel, lemon balm, lovage and parsley, are happy in part or dappled shade, while mint, comfrey and lungwort (*Pulmonaria*) will grow well in full shade.

You should also check whether your soil is acid or alkaline, because again that will determine which herbs will thrive and which will struggle. Most herbs can cope with neutral or slightly acid soil, though some don't do well on alkaline soils – chalk or limestone – such as comfrey (*Symphytum*), sorrel (*Rumex*) and sweet cicely (*Myrrhis odorata*). Those that do like limy conditions include catmint (*Nepeta*), chicory (*Cichorium intybus*), hyssop (*Hyssopus officinalis*), lavender, lungwort (*Pulmonaria*) the marjoram family and rosemary.

Growing organically

Since you are growing these plants for healing purposes, you will want to grow them organically, free from chemicals which can interfere with their health-giving properties. What this means is that you use no weed killers, no artificial fertilizers, and plant-based insecticides, which do not get into the food chain, only as a last resort. For people who are concerned about the

environment, as well as what they eat, it is the only way to garden anyway.

The essence of organic gardening is that you feed the soil with compost or well-rotted manure and allow the plants to draw their nutrients from there, instead of taking them directly from artificial fertilizers. You control pests and diseases by choosing plants that are resistant to both. Grow them 'hard' by not over-feeding, which makes them soft and sappy and irresistible to pests. It also helps if you grow plenty of plants that will attract natural predators of common pests. Open-faced flowers such as the dwarf morning glory (*Convolvulus tricolor*), nasturtiums (*Tropaeolum*), pot marigolds (*Calendula*) and the half-hardy annual French marigold (*Tagetes*) will attract ladybirds, lacewings and hoverflies.

A few months after planting, the small herb area in the healing garden is already looking very good.

They and particularly their larvae will then feast on aphids with great efficiency, while shrubs and trees with berries such as holly, rowan, cotoneaster and ivy will bring in thrushes which will help control the snail population and other birds to eat insect pests. This will also give you the pleasure of watching birds in your garden and the buzz that comes from being in harmony with the natural world.

Before you start planting, prepare the soil well. Dig it over, removing all traces of weed roots and any large stones. If you

need to improve the drainage for the Mediterranean herbs, add a bucketful of grit to every square metre, along with a bucketful of a nutrient-free soil conditioner such as leaf mould. For other herbs, add grit and compost – just two spadesful to every square metre – instead. On the other hand, if the soil is very free-draining so that water and nutrients just wash straight through it, add bulky organic matter to improve its water retention.

If you have your own compost, that is ideal, but if you have to buy it, make sure it is organic, ideally with the Soil Association's stamp of approval. If you are buying plants or herbs, try to buy those that have been organically grown. If you can't find them in the garden centre, then try a specialist nursery.

Caring for herbs

One of the best ways to keep herbs vigorous and growing well is by regular picking, which of course has the same effect as pruning – encouraging the plant to produce lots of bushy new growth. In very dry weather, water them well, especially those such as mint and comfrey that like it wet – but that's no hardship. Playing the hose on them on a warm summer's evening and releasing the fragrance into the air is a very pleasurable experience.

While herbs by and large are not prone to lots of pests and diseases, they inevitably get some. Caterpillars can be picked off by hand and thrown to the birds. Slugs and snails can be trapped in large yogurt or cream cartons sunk into the soil and half-filled with beer. With the smaller cartons, the slugs and snails seem to drink their fill and clamber out again, leaving slightly wobbly trails. Alternatively use a barrier method – sharp grit, baked crushed eggshells, crushed slate and so forth. With aphids, either squash them with your thumb and finger when you first see them or, if there are too many or you are too squeamish, spray with an organic pest

If you have no garden, make your own small herb garden in a pot. Here thyme, fennel, rosemary and variegated sage are planted in gritty, free-draining compost. Constant picking should keep them small, but if they grow too large, move them into separate pots.

spray, horticultural soap or even just a jet of water. Bay trees often suffer with scale insect. Black sooty mould on the surface of the leaves is often a sign of scale insect underneath. Wash off the mould with soapy water and gently scrape off the scales.

Mint and comfrey can both suffer from rust. Any plants affected should be dug up and destroyed. Alternatively, if your mint is in a space by itself, you can pile dry straw round it in autumn and set fire to it. This kills off all the rust spores, both on the plants, which will produce new, clean growth next spring, and in the soil. Mildew is best prevented by keeping plants well watered during dry weather but, if the plants are affected, soak elder leaves in water and spray with that.

Creating herb gardens

Where you grow medicinal plants, whether in mixed borders or in separate herb beds or gardens, depends entirely on how much space you have to play with, how much you like herbs and how you plan to use the area. If the herbs are primarily for the kitchen – and after all, eating them is an excellent way of taking your medicine, as it were – it makes sense to site them as close to the kitchen door as is practical. Nipping out for a handful of coriander or a few sprigs of rosemary is one thing; trekking to the bottom of the garden for them is another, especially when it's wet or cold. On the other hand, if you want the herb garden to be a fragrant retreat, somewhere to escape to, then a sunny site at the bottom of the garden would be ideal.

You can always grow the main culinary herbs in pots near the back door.

There's no doubt that many of them are very handsome plants, well worth including in the garden for their looks alone. Indeed, some medicinal plants are far more widely grown as ornamentals – the pasque flower (*Anemone pulsatilla*), echinacea, sunflowers (*Helenium*), wild honeysuckle (*Lonicera periclymenum*), pot marigolds (*Calendula*), nasturtium, roses, verbascum – and some culinary and medicinal herbs are excellent plants for a mixed border. Rosemary is an ideal structural evergreen where space is limited. Thyme is perfect for growing on a patio or a path in between paving slabs. Fennel with its very delicate leaves and flat, mustard-yellow flower heads can weave any border together, while chives with their spiky grass-like leaves and striking mauve-pink pompom flowers are a lovely edging. Some people grow them under roses, as the onion smell is said to ward off greenfly.

One herb is best excluded from a border – mint– because it will quickly take over. Grow it in a bed on its own if you have space, or bury a very large pot – even a plastic dustbin – with the bottom cut out in the soil and plant in that. Since mint spreads rooting as it goes, leave 7.5–10cm (3–4in) of the pot proud of the soil to prevent it escaping sideways.

If you prefer, you could create a special border just for your herbs. It could be a cottage-garden style border with everything grown together, though it would make sense to impose some sort of order on the plants in terms of height. Although some herbs give a very good show even in their first season, you might want to fill in any spaces with annuals – pot marigolds (*Calendula*) for example, nasturtiums or dill (though don't grow dill if you are also growing fennel; they cross-pollinate and produce fill or dennel).

If you are going to use them a lot it might be better to compartmentalize them for easier access. You could make a very simple square or rectangular bed, divided into smaller squares with double rows of bricks. If you're not sure how permanent you want them to be, just dig out the depth of the bricks, compact the soil in the trenches as firmly as you can, and lay them on that. If you want it to be a permanent feature, make proper paths, laying the bricks on a dry mix of sand and cement. You could make a herb wheel if you have a spot suitable for a circular bed, using bricks in the same way.

You can make your herb garden as elaborate as you like. You could make a physic garden, with formal clipped hedges defining square or rectangular beds. Box is the usual option, but although it is a healing plant, it is also highly toxic and should never be self-administered. A more useful healing option would be lavender or hyssop – both evergreen and both with blue-mauve flowers. Hyssop, incidentally, was introduced into Britain from mainland Europe in 1597 by John Gerard and rapidly became a favourite for knot gardens with the Elizabethans and early Stuarts. Knot gardens, of course, with ribbons of different dwarf hedging plants woven in and out to form intricate patterns, are another option, but are quite tricky to lay out and take a lot of looking after. The hedges need to be trimmed accurately and frequently if they are to look good.

You needn't limit yourself to just one herb garden if you have space. Medical herbalist Anne MacIntyre has a number of different areas within her large Gloucestershire garden – an astrological garden laid out according to Culpeper's principles, one planted with Ayurvedic plants, another with Chinese remedies, and yet another for lovers (not strictly medicinal, you might think, but what better to warm the heart and lift the spirits and make you feel great?).

Chamomile releases its fresh apple scent when trodden on, and so makes a delightful path. It will need careful hand weeding until the plants are well established.

Angelica archangelica (Angelica)

HEALING PLANTS FOR YOUR GARDEN

FS = flowering season
H&S = average height and spread, given after 10 years for shrubs,
and after one full season for the rest
E = evergreen

Unless stated otherwise, you can assume that the plant likes a moderately fertile soil, neutral, moist but not boggy.

Achillea millefolium (Yarrow)
This plant has been used for healing in many parts of the world for thousands of years. One of its common names, 'woundwort', describes what it's good for, and its botanical name comes from the legend that Achilles used it to heal his soldiers' wounds in battle. It was still used to dress wounds in the First World War. It is anti-septic, anti-inflammatory and astringent. Externally, it's an excel-lent healing remedy for cuts, burns, even eczema. Internally, it's good for digestive problems such as colitis, wind and diarrhoea, for regulating the menstrual cycle, and for bringing down fevers by mak-ing you perspire. It's also a good remedy for lowering blood pressure and improving the circulation.

USE
An infusion made with the leaves and flowers. Externally, to soothe bruises or stop bleeding, press the fresh leaf against the wound.

Do not take if you are pregnant. Do not take in large quantities.
FS Jul–Sep. H&S 30–60 × 60cm (1 × 2ft). Sun.

Alchemilla vulgaris* or *A. alpina
(Lady's mantle)
Its Latin name comes from the Arabic word for alchemy, and its common name from its association with the Virgin Mary during medieval times. It is essentially a woman's herb, used for a range of gynaecological and urological problems. It can also aid contractions during childbirth and so should be avoided by pregnant women before full term. Externally it can be used as a douche, a gargle or mouthwash, and to treat cuts, rashes, even insect bites.

USE
Make an infusion with the leaves and flowers in June or July, or make a decoction with the fresh root.

FS May–Jul. H&S *A. vulgaris* 50 × 60cm (1ft 8in), *A. alpina* 15 × 40cm (6in × 1ft 4in). Any soil except very wet. Sun/part shade. Cut back after flowering to prevent seeding everywhere.

Anethum graveolens (Dill)
Used to get babies to sleep – its name comes from the Anglo-Saxon word *dylle*, which means to lull. It also contains a muscle relaxant, so is good for relieving spasm and tension in the digestive system which cause wind, gripe in babies (it was the main ingredient of gripe water), constipation, diarrhoea and so on. It's also good for hacking coughs and asthma.

USE
Infusion of leaves in summer or decoction of seeds.

FS Apr–Jul. H&S 75 × 30cm (2ft 6in × 1ft). Full sun. Annual.

Angelica archangelica (Angelica)
Antibacterial and antifungal, it's a good, general detoxifier. Use an infusion of the leaves for digestive problems, as a tonic to the nervous system and for menstrual problems. A decoction of the roots is a very good expectorant for coughs, colds and catarrh.

USE
Infusion of leaves and decoction of root, stem and seeds.

Do not take if you have diabetes. Do not take in large quantities.
FS Jun–Aug. H&S 1.8m × 80cm (6 × 2ft 8in). Rich, moisture-retentive soil. Part shade. Biennial, but if you prevent the flowers from setting seed it may live 3–4 years.

Calendula officinalis (Pot marigold)

The flowers are astringent, antiseptic, antiviral, antifungal and antibacterial. Internally, they're good for flu, candida, bowel infections, digestive problems. They improve circulation and, having oestrogenic properties, are good for regulating menstruation and for some reproductive problems. Externally, they are good for cuts, grazes, burns, sores, ulcers.

USE

Infusion of flowers to drink, or externally apply as a compress. Or place a flower in a small pot of aqueous cream until the cream has turned pale orange. Remove the flower.

FS May–Aug. H&S 60 × 45cm (2ft × 1ft 6in). Sun/part shade. Annual.

Chamaemelum nobile (Roman chamomile)

Used by the Egyptians, Greeks and Saxons to cure fevers and to calm people, this remedy is good for stress-related problems – headache, digestive disorders and insomnia. It also acts as an antihistamine to relieve allergies such as hay fever, asthma and ezcema. It has analgesic properties too, and is antibacterial, antiseptic, anti-inflammatory and antifungal. Externally, it soothes a range of skin disorders.

USE

Infusion of flowers to be drunk or used externally as a compress. You can also make an oil by packing flower heads into an airtight jar,

Calendula officinalis (Pot marigold)

covering with oil – olive or grapeseed – and leaving in a sunny spot for three weeks. Squeeze it through a muslin bag and store.

FS Jun–Jul. H&S 15 × 30cm (6in × 1ft). E. Full sun.

Coriandrum sativum (Coriander)

Used in every ancient civilization, it is good for digestive orders, including those that are stress-related such as peptic ulcers and for hot, inflammatory conditions such as arthritis and rheumatism, conjunctivitis and cystitis. It helps cool fevers and is a useful muscle relaxant in conditions such as colic and menstrual cramps.

USE

Infusion of leaves and flowers to be drunk or used externally as a compress. Crush seeds to make a poultice.

FS Jun–Jul. H&S 45 × 25cm (18 × 10in). Full sun. Annual.

Echinacea purpurea (Purple coneflower)

Echinacea purpurea (Purple coneflower)
Its healing properties were first discovered by native Americans who chewed the root to quench thirst and relieve toothache (it has a local anaesthetic effect), and took it internally to relieve headache, stomach pain, colds, coughs, symptoms of measles, boils and so on. It is now known to be antibacterial, antifungal, antiviral, anti-inflammatory, and excellent for boosting the immune system to ward off infections such as colds and flu.

USE
Decoction or tincture of the root.

FS Jul–Aug. H&S 90 × 30cm (3 × 1ft). Full sun.

Filipendula ulmaria (Meadowsweet)
It contains salicylic acid – the raw material of aspirin – and has many of the same pain-relieving, anti-inflammatory properties, but its other great healing virtue is that, far from irritating the stomach as aspirin does, it cures a range of digestive problems from heartburn to diarrhoea. It's also a diuretic, an antiseptic and good for healing external wounds.

USE
Internally, infusion of flowers and leaves. Externally, decoction of flowers for compresses.

FS Jun– Sep. H&S 1.2m × 40cm (4 × 1ft 4in). Moist rich soil. Sun/part shade.

Foeniculum vulgare (Fennel)
This is a remedy for digestive problems, a diuretic, an anti-spasmodic and its hormone-like properties make it useful for menstrual and menopausal symptoms. Externally, it also makes a useful eye bath.

USE
Infusion of the leaves or decoction of the seeds or root.

FS Aug–Sep. H&S 1.5–2 × 1m (5–6 × 3ft). Will grow on dry soil, but does much better in moister conditions. Full sun. Seeds freely.

Humulus lupulus (Hops)
A useful relaxant and sedative to induce restful sleep and ease stress-related digestive problems. Recent research has found that there is an

oestrogenic hormone in hops that increases milk flow in breast-feeding mothers.

USE
Infusions made from the female flowers (strobiles).

Do not take if you suffer from a depressive illness. Contact with the pollen of female flowers can cause dermatitis in some people.
FS Jun–Jul. H&S 6 × 6m (20 × 20ft). Sun/light shade.

Hypericum perforatum (St John's wort)
Used by the Greeks and Romans to staunch bleeding in battle, it is still valuable externally for healing cuts, abrasions, burns and bruises and also for nerve pain. More recently it has been hailed as nature's Prozac for its ability to fight depression and particularly Seasonal Affective Disorder (SAD) by increasing sensitivity to sunlight and therefore the production of serotonin, one of the body's own 'happy drugs'. It is good for emotional problems during the meno-pause, and is also antibacterial and antiviral. Research is currently underway into its potential for treating HIV.

USE
Infusion of flowers and leaves or tincture of the fresh, rather than dried, herb.

Check with a practitioner first if you are taking any prescription drugs. Also, do not take if you are sensitive to sunlight.
FS Jul–Sep. H&S 90 × 60cm (3 × 2ft). E. Sun or shade.

Hyssopus officinalis (Hyssop)
This is valuable for warding off infections, particularly of the respiratory tract, by boosting the immune system. An expectorant, decongestant, antispasmodic and antiseptic, it also encourages sweating to reduce fever and clear toxins. Recent research suggests that the mould that produces penicillin grows on the leaf. Externally, it's good for cuts and bruises and, in a bath, helpful for relief of arthritis and rheumatism.

USE
Infusion of flowers and leaves.

Do not take if you are pregnant. If you suffer from epilepsy, avoid

Hyssopus officinalis (Hyssop)

the essential oil.
FS Jun–Sep. H&S 60 × 60cm (2 × 2ft). E/semi-E. Full sun.

Inula helenium (Elecampane)
This plant is antibacterial, antifungal, antiseptic and a useful expectorant for chest complaints. Taken hot, it can bring down the temperature. It also stimulates digestion. Externally, it's a good antiseptic for wounds and infections such as scabies, acne and herpes.

USE
Decoction of the root.

FS Jul–Aug. H&S 1.5 × 1m (5 × 3ft). Moist soil. Full sun/part shade.

Jasminum officinale (Common jasmine)

This astringent, antiseptic and antispasmodic plant is good for problems of the female reproductive system in many ways. It's a relaxant as well, a decongestant, good as a gargle for sore throats and mouths and also for inflammation of the eyes and skin.

USE
Infusion of flowers.

FS Jun–Oct. H&S 7.3 × 7.3m (24 × 24ft). Semi-E. Sun/light shade.

Lavandula angustifolia (Lavender)

This is a very versatile medicinal plant, used internally to relieve stress and tension, to treat digestive problems, especially stress-related ones, and to fight off respiratory infections. It can also bring down fevers, or, as a decongestant, clear phlegm. Externally, the essential oil can calm nerves, reduce stress and aid sleep. It also works extremely well on wounds, speeding up healing and reducing scarring.

USE
Infusion of flowers.

FS Jul–Aug. H&S 80 × 80cm (2ft 8in × 2ft 8in). E. Light, free-draining soil. Full sun.

Lonicera periclymenum **or *L. caprifolium*** (Honeysuckle)

The leaves and flowers both contain salicylic acid – the raw ingredient of aspirin – and so can be used to the same analgesic effect. They are also a diuretic. The leaves have anti-inflammatory and antibiotic properties, useful against chest infections and gastro-enteritis, particularly colitis. They are good for the liver and spleen and have mild laxative properties.

USE
Infusion of leaves and flowers, together or separately.

FS May–Jun. H&S 3.7 × 3.7m (12 × 12ft). Light shade.

Melissa officinalis (Lemon balm)

A favourite with Arabs and Romans, it's good for relieving stress and lifting depression, sharpening the mind and also inducing restful sleep. It's helpful for many digestive problems, especially if stress-related, and can also help to ease symptoms of PMS, and the

Oenothera biennis (Evening primrose)

pain of childbirth. It's good for allergies such as eczema and hay fever, and a leaf applied to the skin helps reduce the swelling of cold sores very quickly.

USE
Infusion of fresh or frozen (not dried) leaves or leaves and flowers.

FS Jun–Aug. H&S 60 × 40cm (2 × 1ft 4in). Sun/light shade.

Mentha × *piperita* (Peppermint)
All ancient civilizations used mint for medicinal purposes. Its relaxant and antispasmodic properties make it a first-class remedy for digestive problems from heartburn through nausea to diarrhoea. Drinking the infusion hot can bring down a fever, but it can also be warming to boost the circulation. It's antiseptic and also a stimulant.

USE
Infusion of leaves.

Do not use on babies.
FS Jul–Aug. H&S 45cm × 1m (1ft 6in × 3ft). Moist soil. Sun/part shade.

Nepeta cataria (Catmint)
Internally, it's a good remedy for relaxing tense muscles, and so relieving wind and indigestion, menstrual cramps and PMS, and is also a decongestant and expectorant. It will bring down fevers too, and bring out the spots in cases of chickenpox and measles. Used externally, it's an antiseptic, and will staunch bleeding as well. It's also good for scalp irritations, and as a poultice for bruises.

USE
Infusion of flowering tips or poultice of flowering tips and leaves.

FS Jun–Sep. H&S 1 × 6m (3 × 2 ft). Well-drained soil. Full sun.

Ocimum basilicum (Basil)
This remedy is good for stress-related problems from headaches to indigestion, for other digestive problems and, taken as a hot infusion, it acts as a decongestant for chest problems. It's also good for the nervous system, aiding concentration. Externally, the leaves can be rubbed directly on minor wounds, stings and bites.

USE
Infusion of leaves.

FS Aug–Sep. H&S 45 × 30cm (1ft 6in × 1ft). Rich, moist soil. Full sun. Shelter from wind. Annual.

Oenothera biennis (Evening primrose)
A decoction of leaves and stems is good for irritations of the digestive tract, but it is the oil from the seeds that is medicinally most important. It contains GLA (gamma-linoleic acid), which has shown in many trials to be beneficial for PMS, for boosting the immune and endocrine systems, protecting against arterial disease, promoting weight loss, improving eczema, relieving the pain and stiffness of arthritis and rheumatism, even helping sufferers from MS.

USE
Decoction of stems, leaves and seeds.

FS Jun–Aug. H&S 1.2m × 60cm (4 × 2ft). Well-drained soil. Full sun.

Origanum majorana (Sweet marjoram)
This herb is good for all kinds of tension and stress-related conditions, from headaches to PMS to insomnia. It's also said to prevent seasickness. It's a decongestant, taken as a hot infusion, a diuretic, and also antimicrobial and antiseptic, since it is rich in thymol. It is also rich in antioxidants, which help delay the physical ageing process.

USE
Infusion of leaves and flowers.

FS Jun–Sep. H&S 60 × 60cm (2 × 2ft). Well-drained soil. Full sun. Half-hardy perennial, best grown as an annual.

Petroselinum crispum (Parsley)
It's a tonic for the nervous system, and good for digestion, stimulating the appetite and combating wind. It's also a diuretic, very useful for urinary infections and fluid retention, as well as helping with such conditions as arthritis and gout. It's a useful herb in childbirth, helping contractions, and afterwards to stimulate the flow of breast milk.

USE
Infusion of leaves, or decoction of root and seeds. A handful of freshly picked parsley eaten raw helps with cystitis attacks.

Do not take if you are pregnant or have kidney disease.
FS Jul–Aug in second year. H&S

Salvia sclarea (Clary sage)

40 × 40cm (16 × 16in). Sun/partial shade.

Pulmonaria officinalis
(Lungwort)
As both its Latin and common names suggest, this is an excellent remedy for lung problems. Externally, it is also a very good remedy for minor wounds, and for varicose veins and haemorrhoids.

USE
Infusion of leaves and flowers.

FS Mar–May. H&S 30 × 30cm (1 × 1ft). E. Sun/partial shade.

Rosa canina or any fragrant variety
Scented rose petals, as well as the leaves and hips, have long been used for healing. Pliny the Elder lists thirty-two different medicines made from roses. They are a great tonic for the nervous system, for the emotions and for the spirits, having a calming and restorative effect. They are a cooling remedy for fevers and inflammatory problems, they help to boost the immune system, and are good for a range of chest problems. They can also help the flora and fauna in the gut return to normal after a course of antibiotics. Rosehips, a rich source of vitamin C, are good for gynaecological problems.

USE
Infusion of petals or petals and leaves. Decoction of rosehip with seeds removed. Syrup of petals or rosehips.

FS Jun–Sep. H&S 3 × 3m (10 × 10ft). Sun/part shade.

Rosmarinus officinalis
(Rosemary)
A popular remedy for centuries for improving concentration and memory – rosemary for remembrance – and since it works by stimulating the flow of blood to the head, that may well be true. It is certainly good for headaches. It is antiseptic, antibacterial, antimicrobial and antifungal, stimulates the digestive system and the liver, and boosts the immune system. It's also a diuretic, an astringent, and an antioxidant, helping to slow down the ageing process.

Externally, it can be used for healing minor wounds and as a douche and a mouthwash.

USE
Infusion of the leaves and flowers, or decoction of the leaves.

FS May–Jun. H&S 1.2 × 1.5m (4 × 5ft). E. Well-drained, slightly alkaline soil. Full sun.

Salvia officinalis (Sage)
There is an old Latin saying, *Cur moriatur homo cui salvia crescit in horto?* – Why would a man die when he has sage in his garden? It has powerful antiseptic as well as antibacterial and antifungal properties. It's good for the digestion, the chest, the liver and the kidneys, and its oestrogenic properties make it useful for menopausal symptoms, too. Externally, it is good for all minor injuries including sunburn. It's also useful as a mouthwash and gargle, and as a douche against thrush. It may also be good for preventing memory loss (see page 51).

USE
Infusion of leaves.

Do not take if you are pregnant or breastfeeding.
FS Jun–Jul. H&S 1 × 1.2m (3 × 4ft). E. Well-drained soil. Full sun.

Salvia sclarea (Clary sage)
A useful tonic for the nervous system and to relieve many stress-induced symptoms, from asthma to insomnia. It's also a relaxant, relieving painful spasm in both the gut and the uterus during

childbirth. Its oestrogenic properties make a valuable remedy for menopausal symptoms such as hot flushes and night sweats. It can help revitalize people who are mentally or physically exhausted.

USE
Infusion of leaves and flowers. Decoction of seeds.

Do not take if you are pregnant.
FS Jun–Aug. H&S 1– 1.2m × 30cm (3–4 × 1ft). Full sun.

Sambucus nigra (Elderberry)
'The medicine chest of the country people' was how the seventeenth-century writer John Evelyn described elder. An infusion of the flowers is good for colds, coughs and flu by reducing fever, and acting as a decongestant and expectorant. It's also useful for bringing out the eruptive rashes in measles and chickenpox, and as a diuretic, too. It's always been used as a calming remedy, to lift depression and aid restful sleep. Elderberries, rich in vitamins A and C, can be made into a syrup and used as a warming remedy for colds.

USE
Infusion of flowers. Syrup of berries.

FS Jun–Jul. H&S 6 × 6m (20 × 20ft). Almost any soil. Sun/partial shade.

Symphytum officinale (Comfrey)
One of its common names – knitbone – tells you what it does. It contains a substance that stimulates the production of the cells responsible for forming collagen, cartilage and bone. Used externally, it is an excellent remedy for all minor wounds, speeding up the healing process and reducing scarring.

USE
Infusion of leaves only for internal use. Decoction of root for external use only.

Do not take in large quantities for long periods. There is a risk of liver damage.
FS May–Jun. H&S 1.2m × 60cm (4 × 2ft). Partial shade.

Tanacetum parthenium (Feverfew)
Although its name suggests its ability to bring down fevers, it's best known now as a remedy for migraine and other headaches. A bitter herb, it's also good for digestion and liver function. It's an anti-inflammatory too, so can be helpful in treating arthritis and,

Tanacetum parthenium (Feverfew)

since it also acts as an antihistamine, it can relieve allergies such as asthma and hay fever.

USE
Infusion of leaves or leaves and flowers. Bitter tasting, so add lemon balm or mint. Alternatively eat 3–5 leaves in a sandwich.

FS Jul–Aug. H&S 60 × 30cm (2 × 1ft). Well-drained soil. Full sun. Seeds everywhere.

Thymus vulgaris (Thyme)
A powerful antiseptic, thyme boosts the immune system and fights off infections of the digestive, respiratory and genitourinary systems. It's good for coughs of all types, acting as a muscle relaxant, an expectorant and cooling agent, bringing down any associated fever. It also helps digestion, boosts the function of the liver and is a useful diuretic. It can help with menstrual problems

and recent research has shown that it may play an important role in the function of polyunsaturated fatty acids, which help slow down the physical ageing process.

USE
Infusion of leaves or leaves and flowers.

Do not take if you are pregnant. The essential oil by itself is toxic and should be taken internally only by prescription. Remedies made from the whole plant are safe.

Arctium lappa (Burdock)

FS Jun–Aug. H&S 20 × 30cm (8 × 12in). E. Well-drained, slightly alkaline soil. Full sun.

Tropaeolum majus (Nasturtium)
The peppery leaves are an excellent stimulant to the appetite, the digestion and the liver. It's a useful blood cleanser, and also a diuretic which, along with its antimicrobial properties, makes it useful for urinary infections. It is high in vitamin C, so is an excellent remedy for coughs and colds, and its high iron content helps counter anaemia.

USE
Infusion of the leaves. Eat leaves raw in salads or cooked in soups. FS Jul–Sep. H&S 3 × 1.5m (10 × 5ft). Poor soil. Sun/part shade.

Valeriana officinalis (Valerian)
The root from two-year-old plants is a valuable sedative and remedy for the nervous system. Its relaxant effect also works on smooth muscle such as gut and uterus and can alleviate many stress-related conditions – irritable bowel, period pain, tension headaches, even ME. It can also lower blood pressure. Taken hot, it can induce sweating and so reduce fever, while taken cool it is a diuretic.

USE
Decoction of the two-year-old root or cold infusion of crushed dried root.

Do not take large doses over a long period.
FS Jun–Aug. H&S 1.2 × 1m (4 × 3ft). Well-drained soil. Sun/partial shade.

Verbena officinalis (vervain)
It acts as a tonic to the nervous system, lifts depression and helps relieve many stress-related conditions. It's good for digestion and, as a bitter herb, relieves 'liverish' symptoms such as bilious headaches, constipation and irritability. It's thought to be helpful with migraines. A hot infusion can bring down fevers, while drunk cool it's a diuretic. Since it can stimulate uterine contractions, it is best avoided in pregnancy. After the birth, though, it helps stimulate the flow of milk.

USE
Infusion of leaves and flowers.

Do not take if you are pregnant.
FS Jul–Sep. H&S 60 × 50cm (2 ×
1ft 8in). Full sun.

WILD PLANTS

Long before people had gardens in
which to grow their medicinal
plants, they would harvest them
from the wild. These days most of
us, apart from the most fantast-
ically tidy-minded gardeners, have a
few wild plants – or weeds – in our
gardens, and it's somehow very
reassuring to know that what we
consider to be 'the enemy' for most
of the time does in fact have a useful
purpose. It may not be possible in a
small garden, but if you have room
for a wild area you can grow some
of these plants. Otherwise take
advantage of them if they appear.

Arctium lappa (Burdock)
A decoction of the root makes a
good remedy for digestive and liver
problems. It is also antibacterial
and antifungal but useful too for
re-establishing the right bacterial
balance in the gut after a course of
antibiotics. It is also recommended
for inflammatory conditions such
as gout, arthritis and some skin diseases, including acne. It can also
help with diabetes by lowering
blood sugar levels. A hot tea brings
down fevers.

USE
Infusion of the leaves or decoction
of the root and of the seeds.
FS Jul–Sep. H&S 1.5 × 1m (5 ×
3ft). Partial shade.

Galium aparine (Cleevers or goose grass)
An old country remedy for losing
weight, this is an excellent tonic,
reducing inflammation and clearing toxins. It's very good for the
lymphatic system, and helps with a
range of conditions from eczema
and acne to urinary infections,
gout and arthritis. It's also beneficial for the digestion and the liver.

USE
Infusion of the leaves and flowers.

FS Jun–Sep. H&S 1.2 × 3m (4 ×
10ft). Partial shade.

Plantago major (Greater plantain)
An infusion of the leaves is soothing for inflammations of the digestive, respiratory or urinary systems.
It can stem both internal and external bleeding, as well as encouraging
healing, and is also good for some
allergies. It is antiseptic and, externally, a fresh leaf offers speedy
relief against insect bites or stings.

USE
Infusion of the leaves.

FS Jun-Sep. H&S 12 × 10cm (5 ×
4in). Full sun.

Taraxacum officinale (Dandelion)
Perhaps best known for its diuretic
properties (one of its common
names is 'piss-the-bed'). It is certainly a valuable cleansing tonic,
since unlike many other diuretics it
is a rich source of potassium, and
so replaces that lost from the body
in the urine. Its root is also good

Galium aparine (Cleevers or goose grass)

for the liver and the digestion. The
white latex produced from the
stem is a good treatment for warts,
verrucas and corns.

USE
Infusion of the leaves or decoction
of the root. Roasted dandelion root
is sold in health shops as a coffee
substitute.

No one needs information on how
to grow dandelions!

Urtica dioica (Nettles)
The young leaves make a first-class
spring tonic, stimulating the kidneys to flush out uric acid, a factor
in gout and arthritis, and the liver
to eliminate toxins from the body.
They are astringent and so help stop
bleeding internally and externally
and are also good for allergies such
as hay fever, asthma and eczema. A
hot infusion helps to bring down
fevers and since they are rich in iron
they are good for anaemia.

USE
Infusion of the young leaves and
flowers.

Do not eat old leaves raw.
FS May–Sep. H&S 1.2 × 1m (4 ×
3ft). Sun/partial shade.

The healing power of colour

There is colour in everything we see – in the environment both natural and built, in our gardens of course, and our homes, in our clothes, our possessions, our food, ourselves. It is almost impossible to find yourself in an environment that is all black or all white – even in the most cutting-edge design agency or minimalist hotel – with no other colour at all. And who would want to live in a world that was only shades of grey?

Dahlia 'Chimborazo'

Colour is hugely important in our lives. We are surrounded by it, immersed in it and affected by it even before we are born and our eyes begin to distinguish colours. Light waves passing through the wall of the womb cast a reddish gold light on to the growing baby.

From a very early age we are drawn to strong colours – as any parent knows who has tried in vain to persuade a toddler to choose the tasteful natural wood train rather than the bright red and yellow plastic one. (Many of us still are – just look at the brightly coloured rhododendrons or bedding plants that are snapped up as impulse buys in garden centres!) Ask young children to sort a number of different coloured shapes and until they are four or five they will instinctively sort by colour not shape. They have strong feelings about colour, and can tell you almost as soon as they can speak what their favourite colour is. The wrong coloured toothbrush, beaker

or even sweet can trigger tantrums.

Colour helps us to interpret the world in adult life. Red means danger and stop. Green means go. Red means ripe, green means sour. Brown is live, blue is neutral and yellow and green are earth when you're wiring a plug. And it also helps interpret us to the world. The colours we choose to wear and put on our walls, both indoors and out, send a powerful message to other people. Shrinking violets don't wear bright red or paint their garden fences purple.

Colour reflects our emotions. We 'see red' when we are angry and our blood is up. When we're sad we 'feel blue'. Someone with no personality – no colour you might say – is 'grey'. Grey is a monotone, and 'monotonous' means dull, boring, repetitious and joyless. Someone who is described as 'colourful' on the other hand is full of life and energy, someone who never fails to make an impact. 'Colourful' is almost always used as a term of approbation,

Colours in the same tonal range make for a pleasing, harmonious combination.

although when people describe someone's language as 'colourful', the colour they usually have in mind is 'blue'.

Colour, which as a form of light we absorb through our skin, as well as with our eyes, affects us physically. Ideally we should be exposed to full-spectrum light – that is, natural sunlight or artificial light containing all the colours in the same proportions as sunlight. Many of us spend much of our working day in offices with fluorescent lighting, which contain more blues, yellows and particularly green than natural daylight. Although we can see well enough under this form of artificial light, the long-term lack of natural light can affect our health and feeling of well-being. In the way that some people suffer from Seasonal Affective Disorder, a debilitating form of depression that sets in during the winter months when natural light levels are low, so some people experience similar symptoms from too long spent under fluorescent lights. Often changing them for full-spectrum lighting can help relieve the symptoms.

Individual colours can affect us physically too. Exposure to red, for example, increases blood pressure, heart rate, rate of breathing and muscular activity. It's only a temporary effect, though, disappearing once we are no longer exposed to red. While red stimulates and excites, blue has the opposite effect. It lowers blood pressure, calms the heart rate and reduces tension. It can also help people with insomnia – strong blues being more effective, funnily enough, than pale shades.

If you think that these effects could be as much psychological as purely physical, it's worth pointing out that colours have a distinct effect on plants where there is no psychology involved at all. Research cited by leading colour therapist Theo Gimbel shows that when mustard and cress were exposed to only red light or only green

The vibrant autumn gold of *Acer palmatum* 'Senkaki' is a warm, cheerful colour and reminds us that colour in the garden does not only come from flowers.

light, stunted, bitter-tasting or weak plants were produced, while blue light produced strong, healthy seedlings with good flavour.

Colour also affects us mentally, altering our perceptions. As a result of the different wavelengths of different colours and of the way our eyes and brain perceive them (see page 79), red seems to be closer than it really is, while blue seems further away. Red flowers or artefacts at the far end of the garden will appear closer and so make the garden seem smaller, while blue and grey plants appear further away and, by making the boundary recede, make the space appear bigger.

Emotionally, too, we have strong responses to different colours. Some of them, based on our personal experiences, are individual to us, but in general terms certain colours evoke similar responses in all of us. Our surroundings are certainly more colourful than ever before – encouraged in part by the plethora of home improvement programmes, books and magazines in recent years. Goodbye, magnolia; hello, mandarin, magenta and Majorelle blue. Powerful stuff, and for that reason it's as well to know what effect the colours we are using will have.

In general, warm colours – reds, oranges, yellows – are good for areas of activity such as playrooms inside or areas of activity in the garden, children's play areas or where you entertain. Cool colours – blues and mauves – are ideal for calmer areas, such as bedrooms, while blue, like green, is an ideal colour scheme for the part of the garden where you want to relax, switch off, chill out.

Less cool colours like turquoise and slightly less warm shades like apricot are good for areas of calmer activity – kitchens and dining rooms.

In the work place, in public places such as schools and hospitals, the same principles apply. Green can create a feeling of calm in an otherwise hectic or noisy area, although too much of it can make staff more relaxed and calm than an employer would like.

The philosopher and educationist Rudolph Steiner, who died in 1925, developed a theory of colour for use in the schools he founded around the turn of the last century that is still used in Steiner schools around the world today. The class-

rooms for the five- and six-year-olds are usually pink and red, to encourage emotional security and activity but not aggression. As the children grow, the colour schemes change to include peach and orange and then yellow to encourage their increasing mental activity. Green is the colour for young teenagers to encourage objective thinking and good judgement, moving on to blue and finally violet for the older ones to develop their spiritual side and encourage balance between the physical (red) and the contemplative (blue).

Colour, then, is a very complicated subject and affects us in all sort of ways we may not have considered, so choosing the right plants and hard materials for our gardens is more than just picking up what catches our eye at the garden centre. With a bit of thought, it can be a very significant factor in creating a healing garden.

WHAT IS COLOUR?

Colour is visible light, part of a spectrum of natural electromagnetic energy produced by the sun and all the other cosmic activity

Autumn mist affects the quality of the light and thereby robs the trees of their colour.

Yellow and violet are complementary colours and bring out the intensity in each other. Here *Rudbeckia fulgida* 'Goldsturm' contrasts superbly with *Aster macrophyllus* 'Twilight'.

When sunlight shines through a fountain, the droplets of water act as prisms, showing us the whole colour spectrum.

that takes place in the solar system.

In the seventeenth century Sir Isaac Newton discovered that sunlight, when passed through a triangular glass prism, breaks down into seven colours – red, yellow, orange, green, blue, indigo and violet. These of course are the colours of the rainbow, which is the result of sunlight passing through billions of tiny prisms – raindrops.

It has been argued that Newton included indigo, which is only dark blue after all, as a separate colour to make the number up to seven, a number he and many of his contemporaries believed to have mystical properties. The German scientist, artist and writer Goethe thought in the eighteenth century that there were only six colours: the three primaries – red, yellow and blue – and three secondaries – green, orange and violet. Colour therapists believe there are eight. Certainly if you

look through a prism you can see turquoise quite distinctly between green and blue. If you look at an old stained glass window with the sun shining through it, you'll see that the bands of lead, which hold the pieces of glass in place, are often fringed with an eighth colour – magenta. You will see the same effect if you direct sunlight through a prism on to a piece of paper printed with black lines. They, too, will be fringed with magenta. So not so much the traditional mnemonic Richard Of York Gave Battle In Vain, perhaps, as Richard Of York Gave Terrible Battle Very Mightily.

Visible light is in the centre of the spectrum that starts with cosmic and gamma rays at one end and ends with television, short wave radio and AM radio at the other, with radar, microwaves, infra-red and ultra-violet light and X-rays in between. They are placed in order of wavelength (the distance between successive waves) and measured in nanometres, which are one-millionth of a millimetre. The band of visible light falls between red at 760nm and violet at 380nm. Or, to put it another way, the eye receives light waves at the incredible speeds of between 380 and 760 million cycles per second. The shorter the wavelength, the higher the frequency (the frequency with which the waves oscillate per second), the more energy they produce. So red has a longer wavelength and lower frequency and therefore produces less energy than violet. The fact that light is energy is demonstrated by the fact that even people who are blind can often distinguish colours by the density of air around them. Air over a blue surface, for example, will feel less dense than air over a red one.

What happens when we see colour is that the full spectrum of visible light strikes the object – say a red chair – which absorbs all the other colours in the spectrum except red and that is then reflected back via our eyes to our brain which tells us it is red. You could argue that colour is all in the mind or is a trick of the light. As the scientist John Stewart Collis wrote in his book *The Vision of Glory: The Extraordinary Nature of the Ordinary*: 'We see the yellow daffodil growing up out of the ground and it seems clear that its colour, the most emphatic thing about it, grows up with it, belongs to it. Yet no; that yellow on the daffodil, that red on the rose, was eight minutes ago in the sun.'

In 100 per cent clear, full-spectrum light, the colours we see are always true, but of course it is very rare that the light we experience is 100 per cent clear. It is affected by all sorts of particles in the atmosphere like water vapour – in the form of clouds, mist or rain – and other gases, and of course pollution. On dull, misty days or in heavily polluted places, only a reduced number of light rays can penetrate and the brightness of the colours is drained away. The same thing happens at dusk. As the light fades, so do the colours, and we are left in a world of monotones. All cats are grey in the dark, as the saying goes. That's why white and very pale pastel shades that contain a great deal of white are good in a shady area of the garden or one that you will use in the evenings. White will absorb none of the colours that make up light, bouncing back what little available light there is while darker colours absorb it.

HOW WE SEE COLOUR

Our eyes are extraordinarily complex organs for converting light into information for our brain, which is hugely important in our perception of colour, to interpret. Like a camera, the eye has a lens, which focuses the light, and an iris, which controls the amount of light allowed to pass through and create the nervous

White plants, such as *Papaver somniferum* and *Dictamnus albus*, bounce back available light, making them ideal for shady places or areas used in the evening.

The violet flowers of *Solanum crispum* 'Glasnevin'. Although violet is a mixture of red and blue, it is much more like blue in its effect on us.

But that's not all they do. On the way these impulses also trigger a part of the hypothalamus, the part of the brain which regulates, among other things, the body's internal clock and therefore sleep, appetite and thirst as well as temperature and other involuntary body functions. The hypothalamus in turn also affects the glands that control a wide range of other vital metabolic functions – the manufacture of growth hormone, the function of the thyroid, the adrenals, and both male and female reproductive systems.

Although our eyes are the most important means of absorbing colour, we can also absorb it through our skin. In the same way that ultraviolet light – just outside the visible spectrum – affects our skin and flesh, triggering production of melanin to form a protective layer or tan, so the cells in our body pass on other messages received from the rest of the spectrum to the brain. After all, plants take in sunlight through their leaves – the equivalent of skin – which, in conjunction with water, carbon dioxide and chlorophyll, trigger a very clear biochemical response – the production of food in the form of starch.

In order to process the different wavelengths of different colours, the actual structure of the eye changes. Light that is yellowish-green focuses right on the retina, and so that's the colour we see most easily. Blue light waves, because they are shorter, focus somewhere in front of the retina, which causes the lens to become concave. The effect of this is to push the colour back so that it appears further away from you. Longer red light waves focus behind the retina, and that makes the lens turn convex in order to focus on it, which has a foreshortening effect and seems to pull red closer.

The brain however is much more than a sophisticated processor of information. It also involves memories and emotions, both

impulses which strike the retina at the back of the eye. The retina contains two different types of light receptor cells. The first are cones, which are responsive to the whole range of colours and are most active in the hours of daylight. The other type, rods, are sensitive to the intensity of light, not colour, and are largely responsible for night vision. Between them, they convert the light that enters the eye into tiny electrical impulses that pass along the million or so fibres of the optic nerve to the visual cortex, which is located at the back of the brain. Here the information is interpreted as sight – registering first colour then intensity, tone and form.

of which make our responses to and inter-
pretations of colour unique. We have
favourite colours just as children do,
though we have learnt not to throw a
tantrum if someone else takes the green
winegum. We have colours we dislike for
reasons often associated with memories –
a loathing of dark brown perhaps because
it was the colour of our school uniform or
bright pink because of blancmange we
were forced to eat as children.

We see colours in a subjective way too,
especially as words to describe them are
now involved. How often have you
ordered seeds and grown them only to find
when they flower that what the seed company describes as 'peach', which you like, is
what you'd call 'salmon', which you don't?

Colour blindness

Some people are colour blind. Usually they
have problems in distinguishing red from
green – complementary colours, interestingly – seeing both as muddy browns. A
few can't distinguish between yellow and
blue – again, near-complementaries. It's
widely thought that it's only men who suffer from colour blindness, but in fact some
women do, though fewer of them (about
1 per cent of women compared to 8 per
cent of men). Obviously this is a slight dis-
advantage if you are a gardener – indeed,
some displays you see convince you that
the gardener responsible must be colour
blind! – but you can see all the other
colours clearly enough, and perhaps other
qualities like shape and texture can come
more into play.

HEALING WITH COLOUR

Colour therapy is one of a range of
complementary treatments gaining in popularity these days and, like many of them,
it has in fact been around for thousands of
years. The first recorded mention of colour
used therapeutically comes from an Egyptian papyrus of 1550 BC, which lists colour
cures such as red lead and green copper
salt. It's thought that even semi-precious
stones, like beryls, were ground up and
taken as remedies. It's also believed that
they used coloured light – sunlight shining
through precious stones like sapphires and
rubies directed on to the patient – in temples specially built for the purpose.

Many other ancient cultures from
around the world – Mayan in Central
America, Native American in the north,
Greek, Indian and Chinese – have used
colour as part of healing, too. In Sanskrit
teaching from Tibet, beams of energy
known as chakras shine both in and out of
eight centres of the body. Each chakra has
a different colour, corresponding to the
eight colours of the spectrum, and each is
responsible for different aspects of mind,
body and spirit. The throat chakra for
instance is blue, and affects the throat,
trachea, lungs, the thyroid, the voice,
creativity through sound, channelling,

Wisteria is another
climber with violet-blue
flowers. Like blue, this
colour appears to be
further away than it
really is, so it's a good
plant to use on the
boundaries of a small
garden.

Green is a neutral shade, a calm and balancing colour. A few flowers, such as *Nicotiana* 'Lime Green' are green, but most of this colour comes from foliage.

and the surrender of personal will to universal will.

In Europe, colour was an important part of the doctrine of the Four Humours which was a cornerstone of medicine until the Renaissance. Each humour had its own colour. Phlegmatic (phlegm) was white, melancholy (yellow bile) yellow, choleric (black bile) black, sanguine (blood) red, and practitioners diagnosed imbalances in the humours by the colour of the complexion, the tongue and of body waste.

After the Renaissance, with the ascendancy of science, healing with colour like many other ancient means of healing fell into disuse. The work of Isaac Newton in the eighteenth century on the properties of colour and light, and Goethe in the following century, revived an interest in the subject.

Colour therapy
Colour therapy is a holistic treatment, like many complementary therapies, treating

the whole person physically, mentally and emotionally and attempting to balance the flow of energies within the body. It takes the view that where there is balance and harmony, there is less likelihood of illness, whether it's a manifestation of physical, mental or emotional trauma, and where the cause is external – a virus or bacterium, for example – a person who is balanced in mind, body and spirit is better able to shrug it off.

While there is little hard scientific evidence to show that it works, there is plenty of anecdotal evidence for its effectiveness in treating a whole range of disorders from high blood pressure and migraine to the common cold. It seems particularly effective against stress-related conditions such as eczema and asthma which conventional medicine often finds hard to treat.

Colour therapists use a variety of diagnostic techniques – looking at the aura, dowsing the spine – to see whether there is an imbalance or distortion of colour, checking to see whether a patient is literally 'off-colour'. They also ask questions about patterns of behaviour and mood throughout the day, and take a detailed history including feelings about colours. Dislike of a particular colour through unpleasant associations, for example, may lead to the patient avoiding it.

Once the practitioner has decided which colour is missing or weak, the most powerful treatment is timed exposure to light of that colour. Ideally it should be full-spectrum light shone through good quality stained glass on to patients wearing white cotton clothing, so that the colour passing through to the skin is not altered in any way. Theo Gimbel maintains that it is essential to use the complementary colour too, in the correct proportions. Using just one colour is not nearly as effective, and in some cases can even make symptoms worse.

While light treatment should be carried out by a therapist, there are other less powerful treatments that you can carry out at home – relaxing in daylight under a piece of silk the appropriate colour, for example, using coloured oils for massage or in the bath, or even by wearing clothes of a particular colour. Theo Gimbel treated a patient suffering from the skin disorder psoriasis, which had not responded to orthodox medical treatment. He suggested that he should wear a turquoise shirt next to his skin and, within a few weeks, the symptoms had cleared up completely.

Of course, you can use colour therapeutically in your garden as well, and while inevitably any colour you choose will be diluted by other colours, the one you choose as the main colour can stimulate or relax you, and generally enhance your feeling of well-being.

Not all leaves are green though as the ivy (*Hedera helix* 'Buttercup') here demonstrates.

COLOURS AND THEIR EFFECTS

Red

This is the colour of energy, of love and passion, and also of anger. It is a stimulant, raising blood pressure, heart rate and rate of respiration. It can pick you up when you are feeling lethargic or depressed, giving you a real boost of energy, mental and physical. As a hot colour, it can create a sensation of warmth.

It's not recommended for people under stress since it can lead to aggression. Red is the colour of the chakra associated with the lower part of the body, and reproductive organs, and so is used to treat problems of fertility and sexuality. Pink, which is red and white, appeals to people who are drawn to the positive nature of red but find the pure colour too threatening.

Red's complementary colour on a six-colour spectrum is green. On an eight-colour one it is turquoise.

In the garden, red is a colour for the most active area – the children's play area, for example, or around an eating area. It should be used with restraint in small gardens because too much of it can make the space feel smaller and too stimulating. Certainly not a colour for structures, though terracotta – a much more earthy, natural shade of red – is fine for tiles or pots.

Orange

This is the colour of joy, of movement, and activity in general. It is warm, optimistic, energetic, similar to but gentler in its effects than red. It's a colour to lift depression and overcome anxiety and the effects of major trauma in your life.

Orange is the colour of the chakra that controls the adrenal glands, as well as the lower intestines, kidneys and bladder, so can be used to treat problems relating to those organs. It's a good appetite stimulant too. It's not recommended for people who are already happy-go-lucky, and irresponsible. The complementary colour of orange is blue.

The hot red *Dahlia* 'Tally Ho' glows out of a bed of *Sedum telephium* subsp. *maximum* 'Atropurpureum' like embers in a dying fire.

Above: Blue is a calming and relaxing colour and it is enhanced in this border by the lily-flowered *Tulipa* 'West Point' in yellow, its near-complimentary colour.

Above right: The acid-yellow bracts of *Euphorbia robbiae* brighten up a shady spot.

Again, it's a good warm colour to have in an active area in the garden, and especially where you eat out. A soft orange – peach or apricot – is still warm but a more relaxing option for walls than the pure colour would be. As a plant colour it is warm and exciting. A few shots of hot orange in a predominantly blue planting enlivens it and makes the blues seem even more blue.

Yellow

Another warm colour, yellow is optimistic and stimulating, but this time to the intellect. It helps concentration and the absorption of information, and also encourages the critical faculties, the ability to detach from a situation and review it objectively. The chakra associated with yellow is the solar plexus, which controls the liver, pancreas, spleen and gall bladder, so it's good for regulating and stimulating the digestive system.

Yellow is also said to be a good colour for purging unwanted baggage –

emotional, mental and physical. It is thought to help older people to purge excess calcium in joints which can accumulate to cause arthritis. Its complementary colour is violet.

In the garden, cheerful yellow can be uplifting either as paint on walls or in ever-green foliage, especially on dull winter days, bringing sunshine into an otherwise dark area. Too much or too harsh a tone can be overpowering.

Green

This is the most balanced colour in the spectrum. It's the colour of new life in the plant world and so has become a symbol of renewal and hope. It's also an optimistic colour, but peaceful and calming too, which makes it an ideal colour for relaxation and contemplation. As a balanced colour, it encourages balance in us. Green is the colour of the heart chakra, and can be use to treat problems of the heart – emotional as well as physical – the lower lungs and chest. It counteracts stress,

Right : The vibrant magenta flowers of *Geranium psilostemon*.

Below: *Clematis* 'Bees' Jubilee' has pink flowers with a bright magenta stripe.

but used in excess it may slow you down too much, which is why its complementary colour is red in the six-part colour wheel, and magenta in the eight-part.

Fortunately green is an ideal colour for gardens since it is by far the most dominant colour in the plant world. It's a peaceful, calming colour which can be geed up a bit with the addition of red or magenta, warmed up with yellow, or made cool with touches of white.

Turquoise

This is the colour of immunity, not only in the physical sense, but emotionally and mentally as well. It helps you value your own ideas and opinions rather than rejecting them in favour of other people's, and prevents you from absorbing other people's anxieties. It is the colour of the thymus

chakra – the thymus is the small gland just above the heart, which is partly responsible for the immune system. It can be used to strengthen your immunity and is also helpful for inflammatory conditions. Its complementary colour is red.

Like blue and green, which combine to make it, turquoise is a calming, relaxing colour to use in the garden, good on fences and other woodwork. It's at once close enough to green to blend with plants and distinct enough to show them off to advantage.

Blue

Almost everybody likes blue. While some people like red as much, it provokes stronger negative feelings than blue. Blue is the colour of relaxation and peace. It helps you to think calmly, it slows you down and encourages patience. It has a marked physical effect, lowering blood pressure, heart rate and the rate of respiration – the opposite, in fact, of the effect of red. For that reason it's helpful for insomnia.

Blue is a conservative colour, and is often the choice of deliberate, honest but sometimes introspective people. Blue is the colour of the throat chakra (see page 81) and it's also said to be beneficial for stress-related disorders such as asthma and stomach ulcers. Its complementary colour is orange.

Blue is an easy, relaxing colour in the garden – dark blue on a trellis or fence works well in a formal urban setting, while softer blue-greys are a good choice in small spaces for pushing the boundaries back. As a plant colour it combines well with the colours close to it in tone – pinks and mauves as well as cool silvers and whites – and with its complementaries – orange and its near neighbour, yellow.

Violet

Throughout history, this has been a colour associated with spirituality, royalty and dignity. A mix of red and blue, it takes most of its properties from the latter – it too has a calming effect on the body and is good for meditation, prayer and inducing sleep. It's also good for creativity and is liked by 'arty' people.

Violet is not a hugely popular colour, though, considered depressing by some and pretentious by others. It is the colour of the brow chakra, linked to the pituitary gland, which produces growth hormone and co-ordinates the endocrine system. It is used by colour therapists to treat disorders of the mind and head, and stress. Its complementary colour is yellow.

As a plant colour, it works well with blue, pink and silver and soft shades have a similar misty, distancing effect to that of blue. It also looks good with yellow – think of Michaelmas daisies and golden

rudbeckias in autumn. Its pastel tones also work surprisingly well on woodwork – trellis, arbours and obelisks.

Magenta

This is the colour of purest spiritual energy and of change in the sense of 'letting go', abandoning old ways of thinking and feeling, and old patterns of behaviour that are no longer relevant to your life. It is the colour of the eighth chakra, relating to the pineal gland, which regulates the body clock. The complementary colour is green.

Like red, it's too powerful a colour to be used to any large extent in the bones of a garden, but it's a wonderfully vibrant plant colour for a sunny spot to give a tropical or Mediterranean feel.

The violet-blue flowers of cornflowers (*Centaurea cyanus* 'Blue Boy').

A stunning Kirlian image of the energy field around a leaf.

RADIATING LIGHT

As well as absorbing energy into our bodies in the form of light, we also transmit it. In the 1860s a doctor at St Thomas' Hospital in London, John Kilner, who was in charge of the X-ray department, decided to test the claims made by some scientists and clairvoyants, that they could see a luminous aura surrounding the human body. His invention, the Kilner screen, was a glass screen coated with a dye that made ultra-violet light visible, and through it he could see a blue-grey band of light about 20cm (8in) wide surrounding the body, with a second, weaker band of light beyond. He also discovered that the colour and size of the bands altered according to the subject's state of health and even their mood.

In the 1930s a Russian medical technician, Semyon Kirlian, noticed that while he was giving patients electrotherapy treatment, he could see very small flashes of light on their skin. He developed a method of photography, which uses neither camera nor light to form an image on film, but instead uses the radiation emanating from the object being photographed. He found that every living thing produces a force field of energy which produces a unique pattern in beautiful bright colours, which vary according to which type of film is being used, as a corona around the object. One remarkable Kirlian photograph shows the thumbs of a healer and his or her patient. The healer's thumb looks almost incandescent, a ball of golden yellow surrounded by a ring of fiery scarlet, while the patient's thumb has a blue corona, looking rather like a burner on a gas cooker.

While this scientific evidence was proof for the sceptical that living things are surrounded by a force field of energy, there is no tangible evidence for the existence of a much larger, multi-coloured human aura, which many people claim they are able to see. It is said to be like a three dimensional cocoon – rather like a Russian doll – extending several feet in each direction with layers of colour, starting with very pale magenta closest to the body. That is followed by the eight colours of the spectrum in order, starting with red, and finishing with an outer layer of magenta. Each layer relates to an aspect of the individual, either physical, mental or spiritual, and in a healthy person, all the colours of the spectrum are visible. These layers are not fixed, but move constantly according to external influences as well the individual's overall state of well-being.

For this reason colour therapists, who can see auras, use them as a useful diagnostic tool, enabling them to learn from seeing which colours are out of balance, where the problems actual and potential might lie and what a suitable treatment might be.

Inula helenium produces flowers like the sunrise in summer.

COLOUR IN THE GARDEN

You can use colour in a beneficial way in the garden to affect your mood and emotions and overall sense of well-being. Use it to create different moods in different areas if you like, depending on whether you want to be active and stimulated or relaxed and peaceful. In the way that it's not possible – or even desirable – to use colour in a pure way in the house, so it is in the garden.

Hard landscaping and features

With the desire to use the garden as a room outside, and since we have all become much bolder with colour inside, it's inevitable that stronger tones are being used more and more in the garden. There is a difference, though. Colour outside is being applied in a natural setting – your ceiling is the sky for a start, and there will be plants if not in your own garden then in the surrounding landscape, so you need to bear that in mind when choosing a colour for fences or walls. And you should think very carefully before you start. Just painting the fences maroon, pink or lime green because someone on the telly did it and it looked fun is not a good enough reason! You have to live with it 365 days a year, in the depths of grey dank February as well as the brighter, sunnier (in theory anyway) days of July.

Bright colours foreshorten, so red fences would make your garden seem smaller. Since it's such an energetic, stimulating colour it's not a good choice anyway because even if you are active in the garden, you want to be active in a relaxed sort of way. Dark colours absorb light and again make a space feel smaller.

Pale colours with a lot of white in them reflect light and make the space seem both brighter and larger. Pure white is not an ideal choice for walls in my view. It's fine in tropical or Mediterranean light, but in softer light particularly in winter it can look cold and harsh. Pale yellow, stone, beige even some pale shades of orange – peach or apricot, which are both light and warm – are a better bet.

Since green will be the dominant plant colour in any garden, you need to choose a main colour for the walls, fences and structures that will harmonize with it. Pale shades of green itself, or of the colours on either side of it on the colour wheel would work well. Turquoise/blue/blue-grey on one side, yellow/orange on the other – peach or apricot shades – would all look very good.

The terracotta wall in my own garden seems to change colour at different times of the day or year. It is also an excellent foil for almost all plant colours.

Vibrant royal blue ceramic pots and stools make a bold focal point for this patio area . Although a cool colour, it is such an intense shade that it works well with the equally intense 'hot' colours around it.

Bear in mind that colours look different at different times of day and in different seasons. Across the middle of my own garden, which faces south-east, I have a freestanding, rendered wall painted terracotta. In the mornings with the sun coming up behind it, it is an earthy brown. By midday it's more deep peach and in the evening with the setting sun full on it, it's the colour of blood oranges, and reflected in the long narrow pool in front of it, it makes the water seem on fire.

Although the colours of hard landscaping materials are far more limited than paint colours or wood stains, it's also a factor to bear in mind. Paving materials come in a range of colours. Manufactured slabs, brick, paviours, setts and so forth come in greys, beiges, creams, even red, as do natural stone, slate, gravel and stone chippings.

Incidentally, it's always worth looking at a paving material wet as well as dry because that's how you'll see it a lot of the time, and the colour can change quite drastically. What is a soft buff dry can become a virulent custard when wet.

Decking is growing in popularity as a material for the garden. Different timbers are slightly different in colour, but if left to weather, most fade to a soft silvery grey. Obviously you can stain decking any

colour you like, but bear in mind that it is a comparatively large area, so choose a shade you know you can live with.

In large gardens it's possible to use different paint or stain colours and materials in different areas, but in small spaces it's probably best to stick to one main background colour throughout, and rely on the colour in the planting and the accessories to create different moods.

Accessories – pots, furniture and so forth – come in a wide range of colours now, and of course you can paint them any colour you like. Even something as simple as the colour of the cushions on your garden chairs can set the mood. From this point of view, it's best to stick to either cool colours or hot colours, but aesthetically speaking you can mix the two, provided they are of equal intensity. Scarlet and pastel mauve won't work well together, whereas bright red and bright purple will.

Choose 'hot' colours for the more active areas, where you plan to eat and entertain and where the children will play, and cooler shades for areas where you want to unwind, relax, and switch off.

Colour and plants

When it comes to choosing plants for colour, you have to bear in mind that as

The creamy-white flowers of *Smilacina racemosa* look very good with greens.

well as flowers they all have leaves that are most likely to be green. Since green is a balanced, neutral shade – as is silver or grey – this isn't a problem since it won't interfere with the effect of the chosen flower colour. Yellow or wine red foliage is a different matter and you need to take it into account when making your choices. Indeed, these are plants you are most likely to choose for the colour of their foliage rather than their flowers.

Colour is affected to a considerable degree by the amount of light – colours in full sun look very different from colours in shade where they are not as intense or as luminous. It is also affected by the quality of light. Plants in the soft northern European light look different from those in tropical or Mediterranean light. Pastels, which work well in an English garden, can look washed-out and insipid in a Californian garden, while hot magentas and scarlets which look so vibrant there can look harsh here.

North light gives the truest colour, the nearest to neutral, which is why tradition-ally painters have always chosen north-facing studios, but given the choice most of us would choose a garden that got a bit more sun.

Light and therefore colours are different at different times of the day. Early morning light is cool with a blue tone, the midday sun casts a golden glow over every-thing while the light of the setting sun has a red tone and it affects the colours of plants. In Monet's famous garden at Giverny in France, he planted the bonfire colours – reds, oranges and rich yellows – where they would catch the evening sun and the warmth of their colours would be intensified by the warmth of the light.

Plant colour in a temperate climate is seasonal. In the spring, it is predominantly fresh greens, blues and yellows, with some pink and white from blossom. In summer the spectrum broadens to include mauves

and reds, by autumn golds, oranges, reds and purples predominate, and in winter browns and greys, with just a few splashes of red and gold from berries and bark. By planting for the seasons, you can enjoy all the different colours in your garden at different times, rather than cram in too many at once and have them cancel each other out.

When it comes to choosing plants for colour, you need to bear in mind their flower size, habit and season. Some plants have large flowers that almost cover them, like some clematis. Others have small flow-ers, like helianthemums or many bedding plants, but so many of them that they, too, virtually cover the plant, creating an almost solid mass of colour. With other plants the flowers are much further apart. *Verbena bonariensis*, for example, has flow-ers of intense violet, but they are held in small, widely spaced clusters, so the impact of the colour is far less concentrated.

Obviously length of flowering season is important to consider, too. A plant that flowers for only a couple of weeks is less use-ful than one that goes on for months, although if you plan carefully you can ensure a succession of the desired colour with different plants to take you through the season – bulbs in spring followed by early-, then mid- and late-summer-flowering shrubs, climbers, perennials and annuals.

Bear in mind that for the best therapeu-tic effect you need to include the comple-mentary colour, too – up to a third if it's not a dominant colour, but less if it is. If you wanted an orange border, you'd need at least a third blue, but with a blue bord-er, because orange is so dominant, you would need less than a third.

From a purely aesthetic point of view, the judicious use of the complementary colour in what would otherwise be a single-colour border brings out the essence of the main colour. Splashes of bright red

Right: Fiery *Crocosmia* 'Lucifer' makes a dram-atic 'hot' combination with golden yellow daylilies and heleniums.

with green, for instance, or of violet with yellow, make the greens look greener, the yellows more yellow.

As with hard materials, you need to bear in mind the intensity of the colours. If they are out of balance, the combination does not work anything like as well. Pastel blues work best with pastel oranges – peach or apricot – while strong blues need hot orange.

You'll notice that a colour that hasn't been mentioned at all is white. That's because, in this context, it is no colour and all colours. There are very few flowers, in fact, that are actually pure white – most are very very pale shades of the three primary colours – red, blue and yellow. A 'white garden', as in Kent's Sissinghurst Castle Garden, works so well not because it is in fact all white, but because of all the other colours involved, too – the many shades of green, silver and grey foliage.

White looks good with all pastel shades, especially the cool pinks, blues and mauves, and although patriotic red, white and blue bedding is beloved by many

traditional gardeners, the contrast is harsh and any therapeutic benefits of red and blue cancel each other out.

COLOUR IN THE HEALING GARDEN

Although our garden was to be divided into two main areas, we painted all the fences with a soft green-blue (Cuprinol Garden Shades 'Sea Grass'). We also painted the raised beds the same colour partly because we used two different sorts of timber – untreated railway sleepers and stout 10cm (4in) sawn planks – and painting them the same colour was visually less distracting than leaving two different surfaces. Using one colour in a space like that also helps make it look bigger because there are fewer distractions to divert your eye.

We left the pergola and the decking area in the active part of the garden unpainted. They stretch across almost the whole width of the garden and we wanted to leave the blue-green colour on the boundaries and not introduce it in the centre of the space.

Here, in what would be the most active part of the garden, we introduced hot colours, the colours of fire to reflect the terracotta chimenea, a Mexican free-standing, wood-burning stove, to add a bit of welcome warmth on chilly evenings, and allow more use to be made of the deck. Over the pergola, woven through wires, we used brightly coloured polypropylene ropes starting with red nearest the fire, then orange and finally yellow. To make a screen between the decking and the contemplative part of the garden, we used ripstop, a nylon material used for kites or thin cagoules, which is very light, dries in an instant, and does not fade. It comes in a range of brilliant colours, and you can buy mixed bags of off-cuts very cheaply. To join the pieces, we cut the ends into

The hot orange-red nasturtiums pick up the red and yellow flames painted around the base of the pot.

strips about 15cm (6in) long, and then knotted them together to create a tassel effect. We also used strips of plastic, on to which we glued rich blue glass florist's beads, using a very strong, two-part adhesive. These, like the lengths of ripstop, were woven through horizontal wires about 40cm (16in) apart.

We chose a strong, royal blue to link with the blue planting on the other side, and since it was similar in intensity to the hot colours we also used on the deck, it worked well with those too.

For the pots on the deck, we chose plain terracotta in octagonal shapes, and, to fit in with our fire theme, painted flames around the base and up the sides in scarlet and egg-yolk yellow.

The contemplative area

At the far end of the garden – our contemplative area – we went for mainly foliage planting because green is the most calming, relaxing colour and is good for meditation. It's cool on a hot day and, if you include some yellow-greens, it can also look warm on a dull cold day.

On the fences we planted clematis – *C. flammula*, which has pretty leaves and scented white flowers in late summer, *C. cirrhosa* var. *balearica*, which has evergreen fern-like foliage and small creamy-yellow dangling scented bells in winter, and a twining evergreen, *Holboellia latifolia*, with dark green leaves and clusters of creamy-white scented flowers in spring. The latter is hardy in sheltered gardens.

Yellows and oranges don't have to be harsh. In my own garden, soft yellow *Phlomis russeliana* and burnt orange *Eremurus* x *isabellinus* 'Cleopatra' make a pleasing, gentle combination.

1 *Clematis flammula*

2 *Dryopteris erythrosora*

3 *Bergenia* 'Bressingham White'

4 *Alchemilla erythropoda* (Dwarf lady's mantle)

5 *Anemone × hybrida* 'Honorine Jobert'

6 *Holboellia latifolia*

7 *Dicksonia antartica* (Tree fern)

8 *Pyhllostachys aurea* (Bamboo)

9 *Galium odoratum* (Woodruff)

The evergreens will give us colour and structure all through the winter.

In the two triangular raised beds, we planted contrasting foliage shapes. In the corners, there's *Phyllostachys aurea*, one of the less invasive bamboos, with slender pointed fresh green leaves and green-gold canes – lovely in winter. It's also a good choice for a contemplative area because the wind through the canes makes a gentle rustling sound, which helps mask the noises of the world outside.

In the left-hand corner our main feature plant is a tree fern, *Dicksonia antarctica*, with its long delicate fronds emerging from its brown, hairy trunk rather like a fountain. Tree ferns are very slow-growing, putting on just an inch or so a year, which is why they are rather expensive. In mild gardens they hang on to their leaves right through the winter, but they look pretty scruffy by spring so when the new fronds uncurl from tight, chestnut brown gorilla's knuckles, it's best to trim the old ones off flush with the trunk. Our garden is pretty sheltered, and the tree fern should come through the winter more or less unscathed. They are not reliably hardy everywhere, though, but since their roots are primarily on the outside of their trunks, not in the soil, you can dig them up in autumn, remove the fronds and keep them, wrapped in sacking, in a frost-free place until late spring.

In the other corner our main shrub is *Mahonia × media* 'Winter Sun' with whorls of wonderfully jagged leaves, as well as butter-yellow flowers in winter – very cheerful to look at from the kitchen window, since you're unlikely to be sitting in the contemplative area at that time of year. It does eventually make a large shrub, but it can be cut back to keep it in check.

The rest of the planting is the same in both beds. Evergreen bergenias and thyme along the front, semi-evergreen woodruff (*Galium odoratum*), with a dwarf lady's mantle (*Alchemilla erythropoda*), Japanese anemones and false spikenard (*Smilacena*).

There is a contrast in leaf colour – from pale to bright to deep green – and also in leaf shape. The solid rounded leaves of bergenias contrast well with the small round whorls of the woodruff, and the fans of the alchemilla. Apart from the yellow of the mahonia in winter, the flower colour here is white. The bergenias are *B.* 'Bressingham White', the Japanese anemone, for midsummer to autumn, is *A.* × *hybrida* 'Honorine Jobert', the smilacena, for early summer, has plumes of creamy white flowers, while those on the woodruff in spring and summer are almost pure white. While

red is green's complementary colour, we wanted to enhance the cool calm nature of this part of the garden rather than add any jolts of excitement.

The single-colour bed

As you sit in the contemplative area looking back towards the house, there is a large triangular bed on your left. We decided to make it a blue bed, since blue is a calming, relaxing colour, too. On the fence there is the soft blue clematis *C.* 'Perle d'Azur', which is very free-flowering from July through into the autumn. The planting is mainly perennial, though spring bulbs such as anemones and scillas will provide the colour early on. For early summer, there is the vivid *Anchusa azurea* 'Lodden Royalist' with alpine aquilegias followed by *Salvia* × *sylvestris* 'Mainacht', *Geranium sylvaticum* 'Mayflower', delphiniums – the looser *D. grandiflorum* 'Blue Butterfly' rather than the upright spikes – and steely

The soft blue-grey-green of the woodwork complements the various greens of the foliage.

1   *Clematis* 'Perle d'Azur'

2   *Aconitum carmichaelii* 'Arendsii'

3   *Ceratostigma willmottianum*

4   *Lavandula* 'Hidcote'

5   *Salvia × sylvestris* 'Mainacht'

6   *Delphinium grandi-florum* 'Blue Butterfly'

7   Alpine aquilegias

8   *Anchusa azurea* 'Lodden Royalist'

9   *Echinops ritro*

10 *Eccremocarpus scaber*

11 Bronze fennel

12 *Kniphofia* 'Bees' Sunset'

blue spiky *Echinops ritro*. In late summer into early autumn, we planted rich blue aconites (*Aconitum carmichaelii* 'Arendsii') and *Ceratostigma willmottianum*, the small china-blue flowers of which will go on appearing until the first frosts.

Blue's complementary colour is orange so we also planted a clump of daylilies (for early summer), a delightful, neat red-hot poker, *Kniphofia* 'Bees' Sunset' with soft orange flowers all through the summer, and, for late summer, the soft orange crocosmia, *C. × crocosmiiflora* 'George Davison'. On the fence, there's the ever-green Chilean glory flower (*Eccremocarpus scaber*) with masses of burnt orange tubular flowers with a yellow mouth, from late spring to autumn. It's not hardy everywhere, but if you protect the roots in winter, even

if the frost kills off the top growth it will usually produce new growth from below the soil.

The orange is also a useful link into the hotter part of the garden. Around the deck, in a narrow bed between it and the fence, we planted more red-hot pokers, starting with the dwarf creamy yellow 'Little Maid' at the rill end, and getting taller and hotter the closer we get to the chimenea. As for the pots, in one we sowed mixed dwarf nasturtiums in reds, oranges and yellows, in another, pot marigolds (*Calendula*) in a hot orange, and in the third pot we planted tubers of small bright red dahlias. To grow over the pergola, we planted a vine (*Vitis vinifera*) which would give us grapes eventually and a blaze of fiery colours in autumn.

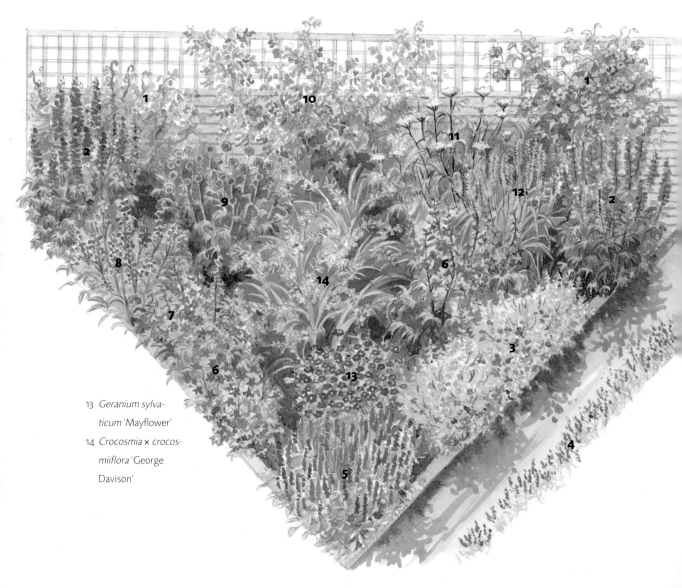

13 *Geranium sylvaticum* 'Mayflower'

14 *Crocosmia × crocosmiiflora* 'George Davison'

Left: The pale blue
flowers of *Ceanothus*
'Puget Blue'.

COLOUR ANALYSIS OF YOUR OWN GARDEN

If you decide you want to use colour in a more controlled way in your own garden, you might find it helpful to do an analysis of the way it looks now.

Look at the colour in it now. Are particular colours concentrated in particular areas or are they dotted about everywhere? Are you happy with the way it looks? If not, grouping the colours either to tone with or be complementary to their neighbours would work better and create areas within the space that are different in mood.

Are there hot colours like red at the far end of the garden? Try moving them closer to the house and replacing them with blues and greys to make the space appear larger. If you're not sure which colours would be best where, experiment with pieces of coloured cloth or paper on bamboo canes and check the effect from the house.

Look at the garden at different times of day. See where the sun falls at different times, and how the changing light affects the colour. Choose plants whose colours will be enhanced by the light at that time of day.

Look at the garden through the seasons, too, noting the changing colours in different areas of the garden. Concentrating early spring colour in one area, for example, will have more impact than dotting it throughout the plot.

Look at your boundaries. Are they all the same or have sections been added at different times so that they are different colours or materials? Painting or staining them all the same colour – a soft, plant-friendly shade, ideally – will make the garden look more cohesive, immediately.

What about your containers? Are they a mixed collection of materials and colours? Again, painting them all the same colour will add unity to the overall look.

Below: The cheerful
yellow flowers of
Clematis orientalis 'Bill
MacKenzie' would be a
good choice for a mainly
violet or blue border.

Crocosmia 'Lucifer'

PLANT LISTS

FS = flowering season
H&S = average height and spread, given after 10 years for trees and shrubs, and after one full season for the rest
E = evergreen

Unless stated otherwise, you can assume that the plant likes a moderately fertile soil, neutral, moist but not boggy.

RED

Winter
BARK
***Cornus alba* 'Elegantissima'**
Bright red stems in winter if pruned hard each spring. Green/cream variegated leaves Apr–Oct. H&S 2 × 1.2m (6 × 4ft). Sun/part shade.

***Salix alba* subsp. *vitellina* 'Britzensis'**
Carmine/scarlet stems, if pruned hard in spring. H&S 1.5m × 90cm (5 × 3ft). Part shade.

Salix alba subsp. *vitellina* 'Britzensis'

BERRIES
***Malus* 'Red Sentinel'**
Glossy red fruit Oct–Mar. White flowers Apr–May. H&S 6 × 3m (20 × 10ft). Full sun.

***Pyracantha* 'Mohave'**
Small orange-red berries Nov–Jan. White flowers May. E. H&S 3.5 × 2m (12 × 6ft). Sun/part shade.

Skimmia japonica
Red berries Oct–Dec. White flowers Apr–May. E. H&S 60 × 60cm (2 × 2ft). Full sun/part shade.

FLOWERS
***Camellia japonica* 'Adolphe Audusson'**
FS Feb–April. Semi-double blood red flowers, yellow stamens. E. H&S 2 × 2m (6 × 6ft). Acid soil. Part shade.

Spring
FLOWERS
***Rhododendron* 'Elizabeth'**
FS Mar–Apr. H&S 80 × 90cm (2ft 8in × 3ft). E. Acid soil. Full sun/part shade.

***Tulipa* 'Showwinner'**
FS Mar–Apr. H&S 20 × 15cm (8 × 6in). Full sun.

FOLIAGE
***Photinia* × *fraseri* 'Red Robin'**
New red growth Oct, brightening through to Mar. E. H&S 2 × 3m (6 × 10ft). Neutral/acid soil. Full sun/part shade.

***Pieris* 'Forest Flame'**
Scarlet growth Mar. White flowers May–Jun. E. H&S 1.2 × 2m (4 × 6ft). Acid soil. Part shade.

Summer
FLOWERS
***Clematis* 'Niobe'**
FS May–Jul. Large ruby flower, yellow anthers. H&S 3.7 × 3.7m (12 × 12ft). Full sun/part shade.

***Clematis* 'Gravetye Beauty'**
FS Jul–Sep. Small ruby flower. H&S 3 × 3m (10 × 10ft). Full sun/part shade.

***Crocosmia* 'Lucifer'**
FS Jul–Sep. H&S 90 × 60cm (3 × 2ft). Full sun/part shade.

***Impatiens* 'Accent Red'**
FS Jun –Sep. H&S 20 × 20cm (8 × 8in). Likes sun but tolerates shade.

***Papaver* 'Beauty of Livermere'**
FS Jun–Jul. Crimson petals. H&S 90 × 50cm (3ft × 1ft 8in). Full sun.

Dahlia 'Bishop of Llandaff'

Pelargonium 'Pulsar Scarlet'
FS Jun–Sep. Single crimson red flowers. H&S 35 × 30cm (14 × 12in). Sun.

Potentilla 'Gibson's Scarlet'
FS May–Aug. Scarlet flowers. H&S 45 × 60cm (1ft 6in × 2ft). Full sun/part shade.

Rosa 'Parkdirektor Riggers'
FS Jul–Sep. Single deep red flowers. H&S 4.6 × 4.6m (15 × 15ft). Full sun/part shade.

Rosa 'Top Marks'
FS Jul–Sep. Double vermilion flowers. H&S 60 × 60cm (2 × 2ft). Full sun/part shade.

Salvia splendens 'Scarlet King'
FS Jun–Sep. H&S 25 × 25cm (10 × 10in). Sun.

Autumn
FLOWERS
Dahlia 'Bishop of Llandaff'
FS Aug–Sep. Dark black-red foliage. H&S 1m × 45cm (3ft × 1ft 6in). Full sun.

Lobelia 'Queen Victoria'
FS Jul–Sep. Purple foliage. H&S 90 × 30cm (3 × 1ft). Moist soil. Full sun/part shade.

Canna 'Roi Humbert'
FS Aug–Sep. Bright orange-red flowers, purple foliage. H&S 1.8m × 50cm (6ft × 20in). Full sun.

Protection over winter.

FOLIAGE
Cotinus 'Grace'
Purple-red leaves, turn scarlet Sep–Oct. Pink flowers Jun–Jul. H&S 3 × 3m (10 × 10ft). Full sun.

Euonymus alatus
Scarlet leaves Sep–Oct. Small yellow flower Apr–May. Pink hanging fruits Sep. H&S 1.5 × 2m (5 × 6ft). Full sun/part shade.

Parthenocissus tricuspidata 'Veitchii'
Crimson-scarlet leaves Sep–Oct. H&S 4.6 × 4.6m (15 × 15ft). Full sun/light shade.

ORANGE

Winter

BARK

Cornus sibirica 'Winter Flame'
Red, orange and yellow stems if pruned hard each spring. H&S 2 × 1.2m (6 × 4 ft). Sun/part shade.

BERRIES

Cotoneaster × suecicus 'Coral Beauty'
Orange-red berries Sep–Nov. Small white flowers Apr–May. Orange leaves Sep–Oct. H&S 1 × 2m (3 × 6ft). Full sun/part shade.

Iris foetidissima
Berries Oct–Dec. Darker veined,

Hamamelis × intermedia 'Jelena'

lilac flowers May–Jun. E. H&S 60 × 75cm (2 × 2ft 6in). Sun/part shade.

Pyracantha 'Orange Glow'
Small berries Sep–Feb. White flowers May–Jun. E. H&S 3.5 × 2.5m (12 × 6ft). Full sun/part shade.

FLOWERS

Hamamelis × intermedia 'Jelena'
FS Dec–Jan. Coppery-orange flowers. Orange-red foliage Sep–Oct. H&S 3 × 4m (10 × 13ft). Neutral to acid soil. Full sun/light shade.

FOLIAGE

Erica carnea 'Foxhollow'
Yellow foliage, orange-red Dec–Feb. E. H&S 20 × 40cm (8 × 16in). Acid soil. Full sun.

Spring

FLOWERS

Berberis darwinii
FS Apr–May. E. H&S 2.2 × 2m (7 × 6ft). Full sun/part shade.

Crocus ancyrenis
FS Feb–Mar. H&S 7 × 5cm (3 × 2in). Well-drained, rich soil. Full sun.

Meconopsis cambrica var. aurantiaca
FS May–Aug. Yellow-orange flower. H&S 30 × 30cm (1 × 1ft) Neutral to acid soil. Sun/part shade.

Rhododendron 'Glowing Embers'
FS Apr–May. H&S 2 × 2m (6 × 6ft). Acid soil. Full sun/part shade.

Tulipa orphanidea Whittalli Group
FS Apr–May. Orange-bronze flowers. H&S 35 × 15cm (14 × 6in). Full sun.

Summer

FLOWERS

Calendula officinalis
FS Jun–Sep. H&S 60 × 20cm (24 × 8in). Sun.

Eccremocarpus scaber
FS Jun–Sep. E. H&S 1.8 × 1.8m (6 × 6ft) after one year. Full sun/light shade.

Eschscholzia californica 'Inferno'
FS Jun–Sep. Orange-scarlet flowers. H&S 25 × 15cm (10 × 6in). Sun.

Kniphofia 'Bees' Sunset'
FS May–Jul. E. H&S 90 × 60cm (3 × 2ft). Sun/part shade.

Lonicera sempervirens
FS Jul–Sep. Scarlet-orange flowers. Semi-E. H&S 4 × 4m (13 × 13ft). Sun/part shade. Prune to 2–3 buds of last season's growth.

Potentilla fruticosa 'Tangerine'
FS Jun–Sep. Orange-yellow flowers. H&S 80 × 80cm (2ft 6in × 2ft 6in). Part shade.

Rosa 'Warm Welcome'
FS Jul–Sep. Semi-double orange-red flowers. H&S 2.2 × 2.2m (7 × 7ft). Full sun.

Tropaeolum majus 'Gleaming Apricots'
FS Jun–Sep. Semi-double peach flowers. H&S 15 × 40cm (6 × 16in). Sun.

Autumn

FLOWERS

Canna 'Wyoming'
FS Aug–Sep. Purple foliage. H&S
1.8m × 50cm (6ft × 1ft 8in). Full
sun. Winter protection needed.

Crocosmia 'Emily McKenzie'
FS Aug–Sep. Darker throat
markings. H&S 60 × 45cm
(2ft × 1ft 6in). Sun/part shade.

Dahlia 'David Howard'
FS Aug–Sep. Bronze-orange
flowers. H&S 1.2m × 90cm (4 ×
3ft). Full sun.

Phygelius × rectus 'Devil's Tears'
FS Aug–Sep. Orange red flowers,
yellow throats. H&S 2 × 2m (6 ×
6ft). Full sun.

FOLIAGE

Amelanchier lamarckii
Scarlet-orange foliage Sep–Oct.
White flowers Apr–May. H&S 5 ×
5m (16 × 16ft). Sun/part shade.

Cercidiphyllum japonicum
Orange-red foliage Sep–Oct. H&S
7 × 7m (22 × 22ft). Sun/part shade.

Fothergilla major
Red, orange and yellow foliage
Sep–Oct. Fragrant white stamens,
no petals– Apr–May. H&S 2 × 2m
(6 × 6ft). Acid soil. Sun/light shade.

YELLOW

Winter

BARK

Cornus stolonifera 'Flaviramea'
Yellow-green stems Nov–Feb, if
pruned hard Feb–Mar. White
flowers on unpruned shrubs. H&S
2.5 × 3m (8 × 10ft). Full sun.

BERRIES

Pyracantha 'Soleil d'Or'
Deep yellow fruit Nov–Jan. White
flowers May. E. H&S 3.5 × 2m
(12 × 6ft). Sun/part shade.

FLOWERS

Hamamelis mollis
FS Jan–Feb. Lemon-yellow flowers.
Yellow-orange foliage Sep–Oct.
H&S 3 × 4m (10 × 13ft). Neutral to
acid soil. Sun/light shade.

Jasminum nudiflorum
FS Nov–Feb. H&S 2 × 2m
(6 × 6ft). Sun/medium shade.

Mahonia × media 'Charity'
FS Dec–Mar. Fragrant lemon-
yellow flowers. E. H&S 3 × 1.8m
(10ft × 5ft 6in). Sun/part shade.

FOLIAGE

Choisya ternata 'Sundance'
White scented flowers. E. H&S
90 × 90cm (3 × 3ft). Sun/part
shade.

**Euonymus fortunei 'Emerald 'n'
Gold'**
Large golden margin on leaf, pink
tips in winter. E. H&S 60 cm ×
20m (2 × 6ft). Full sun.

Hedera helix 'Buttercup'
Bright golden foliage Oct–Mar. E.
H&S 4.9 × 4.9m (16 × 16ft).
Sun/part shade.

Thuja plicata 'Stoneham Gold'
Bright golden foliage May–Jun. E.
H&S 90 × 90cm (3 × 3ft). Full sun.

Jasminum nudiflorum

Spring

FLOWERS

Caltha palustris
FS Apr–May. Semi-E. H&S
30 × 45cm (12 × 16in). Rich, boggy
soil. Full sun. May be grown as a
marginal.

Cytisus × praecox 'Allgold'
FS Apr–May. Golden yellow
flowers. H&S 1 × 1.5m (3 × 5ft).
Full sun.

**Doronicum orientale
'Magnificum'**
FS Apr–May. Large yellow
daisy-like flowers. H&S 90 × 60cm
(3 × 2ft). Sun/part shade.

Anthemis tinctoria 'E. C. Buxton'

Euphorbia polychroma
FS Apr–May. Sulphur-yellow bracts. H&S 45 × 60cm (18in × 2ft). Sun/part shade.

Forsythia × intermedia
FS Apr–May. H&S 3.5 × 2.5m (12 × 8ft). Sun/medium shade.

Tulipa tarda
FS Apr–May. Yellow flowers, white

Rosa 'Graham Thomas'

tips. H&S 15 × 7cm (6 × 3in). Full sun/light shade.

FOLIAGE

Berberis thunbergii 'Aurea'
Lime-yellow leaves. White-tinged pink flowers Mar–Apr. Small glossy red fruit Sep–Oct. H&S 1.5 × 1.5m (5 × 5ft). Sun/part shade.

Hakonechloa macra 'Aureola'
Bright yellow leaves with narrow green stripes. Pale green flower spikes Aug–Sep. H&S 35 × 40cm (14 × 16in). Sun/part shade.

Milium effusum 'Aureum'
Tiny yellow flowers Apr–May. E. H&S 38 × 45cm (15 × 18in). Light shade.

Spiraea japonica 'Goldflame'
New foliage, orange-apricot Apr–May, turning golden yellow. Dark pink flowers May–Jul. H&S 60 × 70cm (2 × 2ft). Sun/light shade.

Summer

FLOWERS

Achillea filipendulina 'Gold Plate'
FS Jul–Sep. H&S 1.2m × 60cm (4 × 2ft). Full sun.

Anthemis tinctoria 'E. C. Buxton'
FS Jun–Aug. Yellow daisy flowers. H&S 90 × 60cm (3 × 2ft). Full sun.

Genista 'Lydia'
FS Apr–May. H&S 60cm × 2m (2 × 6ft). Full sun.

Hemerocallis 'Stella de Oro'
FS Jun–Sep. H&S 30 × 30cm (1 × 1ft). Full sun.

Hypericum 'Hidcote'
FS Jun–Sep. Semi-E. H&S 1 × 1m (3 × 3ft). Light shade.

Lonicera periclymenum 'Graham Thomas'
FS Jul–Sep. Scented yellow flowers. H&S 3.7 × 3.7m (12 × 12ft). Sun/medium shade.

Phlomis russeliana
FS Jun–Aug. Pale yellow hooded flowers. E. H&S 1 × 1.2m (3 × 4ft). Dry open soil. Full sun.

Potentilla fruticosa 'Elizabeth'
FS Jul–Sep. Canary-yellow flowers. H&S 1.2 × 1.2m (4 × 4ft). Sun/medium shade.

FOLIAGE
Humulus lupulus 'Aureus'
Papery female flowers Aug–Sep. H&S 6 × 6m (20 × 20ft). Neutral to acid soil. Medium/light shade.

Autumn
BERRIES
Pyracantha 'Soleil d'Or'
See Winter Berry section, page 103

Sorbus 'Joseph Rock'
Yellow-orange berries Sep–Oct. White flowers Apr–May. Orange-yellow autumn colour. H&S 5 × 2.5m (16 × 8ft). Full sun.

FLOWERS
Clematis 'Bill MacKenzie'
FS Aug–Sep. Small tufted silver seedheads follow. H&S 3.7 × 3.7m (12 × 12ft). Soil with a high organic content. Full sun/light shade.

Rosa 'Graham Thomas'
FS Jul–Sep. Large double flowers. H&S 1.2 × 1.5m (4 × 5ft). Sun/light shade.

Rudbeckia fulgida var. sullivanti 'Goldsturm'
FS Jul–Sep. H&S 75 × 60cm (2.5 × 2ft). Sun/part shade.

FOLIAGE
Acer palmatum 'Sango-kaku'
Yellow leaves Sep–Oct. Small red flowers Mar–Apr. Coral-red winter stems. H&S 2 × 1.2m (6 × 4ft). Neutral to acid soil. Light shade.

Ginkgo biloba
Butterfly-shaped leaves turn yellow Sep–Oct. In male plant, yellow catkins appear same time as leaves. Female flowers after a hot summer, rarely fruits in Britain. H&S 2 × 2.4m (8 × 8ft). Full sun/shade.

GREEN

Winter/Autumn
FLOWERS
Euphorbia amygdaloides var. robbiae
FS Apr–May. Lime-green flowers. E. H&S 60 × 60cm (2 × 2ft). Sun/medium shade.

FOLIAGE
Most conifers and other evergreens.

Spring
FLOWERS
Helleborus argutifolius
FS Apr–May. E. H&S 60 × 60cm (2 × 2ft). Sun/part shade.

Tulipa viridiflora
FS Apr–May. H&S 45 × 20cm (18 × 8in). Full sun.

FOLIAGE
Alchemilla mollis
FS May–Jun. Lime-green flowers. H&S 30 × 60cm (1 × 2ft). Sun/part shade.

Helleborus argutifolius

Dicksonia antarctica
Bright green fronds unfurl in spring. Very slow-growing – 2.5cm (1in) a year – so height and spread are virtually as you buy them. Part shade/shade.

Galium odoratum
FS May–Jun. Scented white flowers. H&S 30 × 60cm (1 × 2ft). Part shade.

Hosta sieboldiana 'Frances Williams'
Blue-green leaves, green-yellow margins. Lilac-white flowers Jul–Aug. H&S 60 × 90cm (2 × 3ft). Moist soil. Part/deep shade.

Salvia patens

Summer

FLOWERS

Angelica archangelica
FS Jun–Aug. Clusters of yellow-green flowers. H&S 1.75m × 80cm (6ft × 2ft 6in). Sun/light shade.

Kniphofia 'Green Jade'
FS Aug–Sep. Green flowers, then cream turning to white. E. H&S 1.2m × 90cm (4 × 3ft). Sun/part shade.

Nicotiana 'Lime Green'
FS Jun–Sep. Lime-green flowers, evening scent. H&S 50 × 25cm (20 × 10in). Full sun.

Autumn

FLOWERS

Itea ilicifolia
FS Aug–Sep. Fragrant catkins, green-white, up to 40cm (15in) long. E. H&S 2 × 2m (6 × 6ft). Light shade.

BLUE

Winter

FLOWERS

Chionodoxa luciliae
FS Feb–Mar. Blue flowers with white centres. H&S 10–15 × 5cm (4–6 × 2in). Full sun.

Crocus 'Blue Pearl'
FS Mar–Apr. H&S 7 × 5cm (3 × 2in). Full sun.

Hepatica × media 'Ballardii'
FS Mar–Apr. Semi-double blue flowers. Semi-E. H&S 15 × 20cm (6 × 8in). Humus-rich, well-drained soil. Part shade.

Iris reticulata
FS Feb. Purple-blue flowers, yellow centre. H&S 10–15 × 5cm (4–6 × 2in). Full sun.

Winter pansies and primulas.

FOLIAGE

Acaena saccaticupula 'Blue Haze'
H&S 15 × 45cm (6 × 18in). E. Red stems, brown flower heads Jun–Aug. Sun/light shade.

Picea pungens 'Koster'
Silvery-blue foliage. E. H&S 1.8m × 90cm (6 × 3ft). Full sun.

Festuca glauca
Blue-green wiry leaves. Flower spikes May–Jun. E. H&S 30 × 25cm (12 × 10in). Sun/part shade.

Spring

FLOWERS

Anemone nemorosa 'Caerulea'
FS Apr. 10 × 10cm (4 × 4in). Humus-rich, well-drained soil. Part shade.

Aquilegia alpina
FS Apr–May. H&S 45 × 30cm (18 × 12in). Humus-rich, well-drained soil. Sun/part shade.

Ceanothus 'Puget Blue'
FS Apr–Jun. E. H&S 3 × 3m (10 × 10ft). Sun/light shade.

Clematis 'Frances Rivis'
FS Apr–May. Mid blue flowers, with white centre. H&S 2.4 × 2.4m (8 × 8ft). Sun/light shade. Roots in shade.

Muscari armeniacum
FS Apr–May. H&S 15–20 × 7cm (6–8 × 3in). Full sun.

Muscari armeniacum

Rosmarinus officinalis
FS May–Jun. E. H&S 1.2 × 1.5m
(4 × 5ft). Light, open soil.
Sun/light shade.

Vinca minor
FS May–Aug. E. H&S 15 × 60cm
(6in × 2ft). Light shade. Trim
lightly in Mar–Apr.

Summer
FLOWERS
***Aconitum carmichaelii* 'Arendsii'**
FS Jul–Aug. H&S 1.2m × 30cm
(4 × 1ft). Part shade.

***Agapanthus* Headbourne hybrids**
FS Jun–Jul. H&S 1.2m × 60cm
(4 × 2ft). Full sun.

***Anchusa azurea* 'Loddon Royalist'**
FS Jun–Jul. H&S 1m × 60cm
(3 × 2ft). Sun/part shade.

Centaurea cyanus
FS May–Jul. H&S 50 × 15cm
(20 × 6in). Full sun.

***Clematis* 'Blue Belle'**
FS Jul–Aug. H&S 3.7 × 3.7m
(12 × 12ft). Sun/light shade.

***Delphinium grandiflorum* 'Blue Butterfly'**
FS Jul–Aug. H&S 80 × 30cm
(2ft 6in × 1ft). Full sun.

***Echinops bannaticus* 'Taplow Blue'**
FS Jul–Aug. H&S 1.5m × 60cm
(5 × 2ft). Sun/part shade.

***Hydrangea macrophylla* 'Mariesii Perfecta'**
FS Jul–Sep. H&S 1.8 × 2m
(6 × 6ft 6in). Sun/light shade.

Nigella damascena 'Miss Jekyll'

***Ipomoea tricolor* 'Heavenly Blue'**
FS Jul–Aug. Blue flowers, white
throat. H&S 3–4m × 30cm
(10–13 × 1ft). Sun/light shade.

***Nigella damascena* 'Miss Jekyll'**
FS Jun–Jul. Inflated seed pods
follow. H&S 45 × 23cm (18 × 9in).
Full sun.

Salvia patens
FS Jul–Sep. H&S 45 × 45cm
(18 × 18in). Sun/dappled shade.

Autumn
FLOWERS
Ceratostigma willmottianum
FS Aug–Oct. H&S 1 × 1m
(3 × 3ft). Full sun.

Salvia uliginosa
FS Aug–Sep. H&S 1.5m × 60cm
(5 × 2ft). Sun/part shade.

VIOLET

Winter
FOLIAGE
***Phormium tenax* 'Purpureum'**
Bronze-purple foliage. E. H&S
1.5 × 2m (5 × 6ft 6in). Bronze-red
flowers from Jul–Aug on plants 4
years plus. Full sun.

Spring
FLOWERS
***Aubrieta* 'Joy'**
FS Mar–May. Mauve flowers. E.
H&S 5 × 60cm (2in × 2ft). Full
sun.

Primula denticulata
FS Mar–May. H&S 30 × 15cm
(12 × 6in). Part shade.

Allium cristophii

Syringa meyeri var. spontanea 'Palibin'
FS Apr–Jun. H&S 70 × 50cm (2ft 4in × 1ft 8in). Light shade.

Viola riviniana Purpurea Group
FS Apr–Jun. Semi-E. H&S 15 × 30cm (6 × 12in). Light/medium shade.

Wisteria sinensis
FS Apr–May. Racemes of lilac flowers up to 23cm (9in). H&S 11 × 11m (36 × 36ft). Full sun.

Summer
FLOWERS
Allium cristophii
FS Jun–Jul. H&S 60 × 45cm (2ft × 18in). Sun/part shade.

Campanula poscharskyana
FS Jun–Jul. H&S 20 × 45cm (8 × 18in). Sun/part shade.

Clematis 'Star of India'
FS Jun–Jul. H&S 3.7 × 3.7m (12 × 12ft). Sun/partial shade. Roots in shade.

Geranium sylvaticum 'Mayflower'
FS May–Jun. H&S 60 × 60cm (2 × 2ft). Sun/part shade.

Hebe 'Bowles' Hybrid'
FS May–Sep. E. H&S 45 × 60cm (18 × 24in). Sun/part shade.

Lavandula angustifolia 'Hidcote'
FS Jul–Aug. E. H&S 50 × 50cm (20 × 20in). Light, well-drained soil. Full sun.

Penstemon 'Sour Grapes'
FS Jul–Aug. H&S 60 × 60cm (2 × 2ft). Sun/part shade.

Solanum crispum 'Glasnevin'
FS Jun–Sep. H&S 1.8 × 1.8m (6 × 6ft). Sun/light shade.

Verbena bonariensis
FS Jul–Sep. H&S 1.2m × 60cm (4 × 2ft). Full sun.

FOLIAGE
Cotinus 'Grace'
Purple-red leaves, scarlet Sep–Oct. Pink flowers Jun–Jul. H&S 3 × 3m (10 × 10ft). Full sun.

Heuchera micrantha var. diversifolia 'Palace Purple'
Cream flowers Jun–Jul. H&S 60 × 30cm (2 × 1ft). E. Very fertile, moist soil. Sun/part shade.

Autumn
BERRIES
Callicarpa bodinieri var. giraldii
Purple-pink berries from Sep. Lilac-pink flowers Aug on wood 2 years old. H&S 3 × 3m (10 × 10ft). Sun/light shade.

Verbena bonariensis

FLOWERS

Aster × frikartii 'Mönch'
FS Aug–Sep. H&S 60 × 60cm
(2 × 2ft). Full sun.

**Clematis viticella 'Purpurea
Plena Elegans'**
FS Jul–Sep. H&S 3.7 × 3.7m
(12 × 12ft). Sun/part shade.

Lirope muscari
FS Aug–Sep. H&S 30 × 30cm
(1 × 1ft). Acidic, well-drained,
moist soil. Part shade.

FOLIAGE

Vitis vinifera 'Purpurea'
Purple leaves, turning rich purple
Sep–Oct. Flowers Mar–Apr.
Followed by inedible grapes turn-
ing black Aug–Sep. H&S 4.6 ×
4.6m (15 × 15ft). Full sun.

Callicarpa bodinieri var. giraldii

MAGENTA

Winter
FLOWERS

Daphne mezereum
FS Feb–Mar. Scented flowers.
H&S 80 × 70cm (2ft 6in × 2ft 4in).
Rich, leafy, well-drained loam.
Light shade.

Spring
FLOWERS

Malus 'Profusion'
FS Mar–Apr. Small purple-red
fruit Aug–Sep. Coppery-crimson
young foliage. H&S 6 × 3m
(20 × 10ft). Sun/light shade.

Rhododendron 'Praecox'
FS Feb–Mar. E. H&S 80 × 90cm
(2ft 6in × 3ft). Well-drained,

fertile, acid soil. Light shade.

Summer
FLOWERS

Armeria maritima
FS May–Jul. E. H&S 20 × 45cm
(8 × 18in). Full sun.

Clematis 'Abundance'
FS Jul–Sep. H&S 3.7 × 3.7m
(12 × 12ft). Sun/partial shade.
Roots in shade.

Geranium psilostemon
FS Jun–Aug. Magenta flowers with
black centres. H&S 90 × 45cm
(3ft × 18in). Sun/part shade.

Lychnis coronaria
FS May–Jul. H&S 80 × 45cm
(2ft 6in × 18in). Full sun.

Lythrum salicaria 'Feuerkerze'
FS Jun–Jul. H&S 90 × 45cm
(3ft × 18in). Full sun.

**Petunia surfinia 'Purple' Surfinia
Series**
FS May–Sep. Magenta flowers,
darker veins. H&S 25 × 90cm
(10in × 3ft). Full sun.

The power of flowers

When you think about the pleasure you get from a garden, one of the most important elements is undoubtedly scent. Certainly the rich heady perfume of regal lilies or old roses in midsummer, the drier scent from tobacco plants on an August evening, the fragrance of sweet vanilla from Christmas box (*Sarcococca*) on a crisp January morning and for some people even the smell of woodsmoke from a bonfire on a November day, all add enormously to the enjoyment that your garden can provide.

Lathryus odoratus 'Black Knight'

More and more, scent is a factor most of us bear in mind when planning and planting a new garden – seating areas with chamomile or thyme underfoot, and overhead pergolas or arbours covered in sweet-scented jasmine, roses or honeysuckle. After years when colour was the most important feature of a new sweet pea or a rose, increasingly the plant breeders are responding to popular demand and breeding fragrance back in.

Scent is perhaps the most powerfully evocative of all sensory stimuli and one of the first to which we respond. Newborn babies, whose eyes cannot yet focus clearly on their mother's face, can pick her out very quickly from other lactating women by her own unique smell. Scent triggers memories pleasant and unpleasant, in a very direct and immediate way. For those of us old enough to remember blackboards, that unique cocktail of floor polish, disinfectant, chalk and, very faintly, boiled cabbage takes us straight back to the classroom, and we are six years old again.

Our olfactory systems are highly sophisticated detection mechanisms and while some people have a more acute sense of smell than others, the average person can distinguish around ten thousand different smells. For professional 'noses', whether they are in the perfume business or the wine business, the total is even higher. Our ability to taste depends about 85 per cent on our sense of smell, which is why wine experts judge a wine primarily by smelling it. And that's why, when you have a really bad head cold and your nose is largely blocked, all food tastes like cardboard.

Scent, on the whole, offers a very pleasurable experience – just watch the expression on people's faces as they bend to smell a particularly fragrant rose or lily. And that's why people throughout history have paid large amounts of money for perfumes – to show status, make themselves more desirable, or, in the great unwashed periods in the past, to disguise what must have been extremely potent body odours. The blending of perfumes requires great skill, getting the balance of top, medium and bottom 'notes' right so that the perfume is still as pleasing, though different, a few hours later as it was at the first sniff.

A famous perfume can contain up to one hundred different ingredients. A few come from animals, civet for example, but the vast majority are plant-based – essential oils extracted from flowers, leaves, bark, berries, gum or even wood. The five main categories are floral, green, citrus, woody and spicy (see below). Most work well with others in their own group, but beyond that there are no hard and fast rules. Citrus works well with most florals, but orange is better than lemon with most woody scents. While you are not setting out to be a master perfumier, it's worth bearing these groups in mind when you are choosing scented plants for your own garden (see page 128).

FLORAL
Jasmine (*J. officinale*), rose-scented geranium (*Pelargonium* 'Graveolens' – flowers and leaves), lavender (*L. angustifolia*), lily of the valley (*Convallaria majalis*), mimosa (*Acacia dealbata*), rose (e.g. *R. × damascena*), violet (*Viola odorata*)

GREEN
Basil, chamomile, clary sage, eucalyptus, lemon balm (*Melissa*), marjoram, mint (*Mentha × piperata*), pine, rosemary, thyme

CITRUS
Orange, mandarin, lemon

WOODY
Angelica (seed and root), birch (*Betula pendula* – bark and leaf buds), cedar (*Cedrus atlantica* – wood), cedarwood

Fragrance is one of the great pleasures in a garden, so always bear it in mind when you are choosing plants.

(*Juniperus virginiana* – wood), yarrow (*Achillea millefolium*)

SPICY

Carnations and pinks (*dianthus*), *Viburnum carlesii*, stocks (*Matthiola incana*), bay (*Laurus nobilis*), cypress, fennel seeds, hops (*Humulus lupulus*), juniper berries

THE BENEFITS OF SCENT

The pleasure that scent gives you also does you good. Increasingly, research in the relatively new science of psycho-neuroimmunology (PNI) is showing that if we feel good, if our sense of well-being is enhanced, then our immune system is stronger and we are better able to fight off illness – or, if we do succumb, we're able to recover more quickly. Conversely, if we are depressed, a particular type of chemical messenger in the body – cytokinin – is produced which suppresses the immune system. Or if we are under great stress, another type of cytokinin is produced which overstimulates the immune system possibly even to the point of breakdown. In both cases, the ability of the immune system to function normally is seriously compromised.

Whereas this effect might once have been dismissed as a placebo effect – all in the mind rather than having any physio-logical basis – most people are beginning to accept that when it comes to health, mind and body are so closely linked that such a distinction is no longer very useful. As well-known psychologists Hans and Michael Eysenck wrote in their book *Mindwatching*, published in 1995, 'We simply have to give up the notion of body as opposed to mind and accept the notion of a body-mind-spirit entity.'

Scent also works on a physiological, molecular level, with the scent molecules passing into the bloodstream either via the lungs or through the skin and being carried all round the body. This fact was

An arch of sweet peas, simple and quick to make, presents the flowers at nose height for your enjoyment.

discovered over two thousand years ago by the Greek botanist and healer Theophrastus, when he found that a scent applied to the skin as a plaster or poultice could be detected some time later in the patient's breath. While scent is at its most powerful in essential oils extracted from plants, the fragrance you smell from plants growing in the garden, though less concentrated, works in the same way.

AROMATHERAPY

Aromatherapy is an alternative therapy that is becoming increasingly recognized as having real and quantifiable merit. Many hospitals and doctors are now either employing qualified aromatherapists or training their own medical personnel in its use. Indeed fifteen out of twenty-three medical schools in Britain offer courses in complementary disciplines. The Essex police force is considering offering it to officers, along with other complementary therapies, as a means of combating the stress of the job, and in Europe, anyway, the cost of aromatherapy treatment is covered by private health insurance policies.

Many aromatherapists apply essential oils, which are distilled from plants, by means of massage – itself a very useful therapy for relieving physical and mental stress, which is made even more beneficial by the oils. Others, though, use the oils purely for inhalation, either by means of a

A double border filled with scented flowers and herbs like this one at Hollington Herbs, is a delight to walk through.

The Regal lily (*Lilium regale*) can fill the house with its rich sweet scent if you plant it near a window.

burner, in bath water, applied to fabric – a pillow or handkerchief, say – or from an impregnated taper.

While aromatherapy techniques rely mainly (but not exclusively) on the use of highly concentrated essential oils, growing scented plants in your garden offers at least some of the same benefits. Certainly, sitting your garden on a warm evening breathing in the scent of honeysuckle or tobacco plants can be almost as pleasurable and relaxing as an aromatherapy massage.

Since aromatherapy also works on a molecular level (see page 119), breathing in the fragrance of flowers means that you are also breathing in scent molecules, albeit fewer of them, which not only trigger very direct responses in your brain but also pass through your lungs and into your bloodstream. Research suggests that even in a very dilute form – so dilute in fact that you may not even be conscious that you are smelling anything – these molecules can still trigger a response. This accords with the beliefs of Dr Edward Bach (see page 134) that a flower essence can still cause a reaction in the body even if it is so dilute that nothing is left of the original plant material except its vibration or energy pattern.

There is even a suggestion that the memory of smell can have a physiological effect. It has been found in some people who suffer from epilepsy that smelling lavender in the pre-fit stages can alter the brainwaves enough to prevent an actual fit taking place. It has been suggested that in some patients, merely remembering the smell of lavender is enough to have the same effect.

History

While the popularity of aromatherapy appears comparatively recent in modern times, and indeed the word itself was only coined in the 1930s, it's a practice that dates back thousands of years. As we know, plants have been used medicinally for anything up to 60,000 years, as the recent discovery of plant material buried near a Neanderthal skeleton suggests (see page 40), but aromatherapy seems to have been invented in Egypt about five thousand years ago. Aromatic plants were burnt and the smoke used to cause drowsiness, alter mood or for fumigation, and perfumes (the word comes from the Latin *per fumum*, meaning 'through smoke') were used both medicinally – to heal the living and embalm the dead – and in religious ceremonies. When Tutankhamun's tomb was excavated in 1922 some three thousand years after he was buried, phials were found containing unguents the fragrance of which was still strong.

Aromatic plants were used for healing in other ancient civilizations, too – in China around five thousand years ago, and the Indian subcontinent, in Ayurvedic medicine, two thousand years later. While the Roman physician, Heroditus, recorded the first, rather crude, method of distillation in 425 BC, it's thought to have been the Persian physician and scholar Avicenna, born in AD 980 in Iran and more accurately called Ibn Sina, who found a far more efficient method of distilling essential oils from plants around a thousand years ago. For this reason, perhaps, the oils were known in England as the 'perfumes of Arabia'. He wrote many books and one of them, the *Canon of Medicine*, was used in many medical schools throughout the known world until the middle of the sixteenth century.

In the Middle Ages, when religious orders became the main purveyors of medicine, essential oils and the knowledge about their use, brought back from the East in many cases by crusaders, were widely used, and botany was an important part of medical studies.

Plants – and essential oils – remained an important part of medicine until the nineteenth century when scientists identi-fied the constituent chemicals in many plants and made synthetic versions of them – drugs, in other words. These were in many cases far more powerful than the original source, with greater potential for harm as well as good, and in this new era in which science was king, essential oils

themselves and other plant remedies suddenly seemed hopelessly old-fashioned and were largely dismissed as primitive, even superstitious nonsense.

In the 1920s a French chemist called René Maurice Gattefossé was working with essential oils in his laboratory at the family perfume business when he burnt his hand very badly. He plunged it into the nearest liquid, a vat of essential oil of lavender as it happened, and he was surprised to find that the burn healed quickly with no scarring. More recently, medical herbalist Anne McIntyre cut down some giant hogweed in her garden on a sunny day – like rue, its sap causes painful chemical burning if the skin is exposed to sunlight – resulting in a large burn on her arm. She treated it with lavender oil and, again, it healed very quickly with no scarring at all.

Impressed by his own experience, Gattefossé devoted time to researching essential oils and their medicinal properties, and in 1937 published a book on his find-ings called *Aromathérapie*, thus coining the name. Another French doctor, Jean Valnet, read Gattefossé's research and, as a doctor in the French army, was able to carry on the work, using essential oils to treat wounded soldiers during the Second World War, dealing with not only physical wounds but also psychiatric disorders. His book on the subject, *The Practice of Aromatherapy*, which was published in 1964, is still considered a standard text in the professional training of aromatherapists.

When aromatherapy arrived in Britain in the 1950s, it was largely due to the efforts of an Austrian biochemist, Dr Marguerite Maury. Although she was interested in the therapeutic effects of essential oils applied through the skin by massage, aromatherapy was generally thought of more as a beauty treatment than an alternative medical application.

While that view has changed to a large extent, it's interesting that in other countries, qualified aromatherapists – many of whom are also medical doctors – are allowed to prescribe essential oils to be taken internally, either by mouth, injection or in suppositories, but British aromatherapists are allowed only to apply essential oils externally.

THE CHEMISTRY OF ESSENTIAL OILS

Essential oils, which are contained in the leaves, flowers, stems and even bark of plants, contain a range of different chemical substances. There are different types of alcohols, found in lavender, rosemary, clary sage, peppermint and tea tree for example, aldehydes, found in citrus, patchouli and melissa, esters, found in different forms in lavender, bergamot, neroli, geranium and lemongrass, ketones, found in pennyroyal, mint, jasmine and fennel, and phenols, found in thyme, fennel and oregano among other herbs.

Many of them are highly beneficial, being antibacterial, antifungal, antiseptic, anti-inflammatory, antibiotic, antispasmodic and diuretic, while some are analgesic or sedative, and others are effective at boosting the immune system.

A few chemicals, the phenols in particular, are potentially harmful if they're used over a long period and in large quantities. Some are skin irritants, others are toxic or even carcinogenic, but they are also excellent for boosting the immune system as well as having antibacterial and antiviral properties; so they are best used very dilute, over only a very short period of time, and only by a qualified aromatherapist. Some ketones, such as pulegone in pennyroyal and thujone in mugwort (*Artemisia*), have potentially harmful side-

effects – epileptic fits or miscarriage – so should obviously be avoided in pregnancy, but others are safe.

You are very unlikely to find any potentially harmful oils on sale, but even common and widely used oils such as lavender can cause headaches and nausea in people who suffer from allergies like hay fever and asthma.

Always check on the effects of individual oils before you use them and use them only in the ways suggested. If you are pregnant then you need to be particularly

A carpet of different thymes releases its scent when you walk on it. It's also a magnet for bees.

careful since oils that are normally perfectly safe may have adverse effects.

BUYING OILS

To obtain maximum benefit from essential oils it is very important to use only 100 per cent pure oils of the highest quality. While it is possible to synthesize the elements in an oil, only the real thing has the vital force that comes from living plants. Unfortunately, as the popularity of aromatherapy spreads, so the number of poor quality, diluted or even synthetic oils available in the shops is on the increase – not to mention any number of commercial products on the supermarket shelves from foam baths to fabric softeners which now have the word 'aromatherapy' on their labels, though in many cases that's about all they do have.

It's also worth noting that there are different types of the same oil – oils from different varieties of the same plant will have slightly different properties. *Eucalyptus globulus*, for example, is an excellent decongestant and mental stimulant, but can trigger epileptic fits in young children. For them *Eucalyptus smithii* or *radiata* is safer. The conditions in which a plant is grown – soil type, amount of nutrients, altitude, temperature and so on – will also affect the chemical composition, and therefore the effect, of oils produced from exactly the same plant variety.

A small city garden like this one can be filled with scent from just a few lilies. The walls give off heat, which encourages the plants to release their fragrance.

For these reasons, it is best to buy oils from a qualified aromatherapist if at all possible. If not, look for a very reputable brand, which will have the country of origin, and the date when the oil was bottled on the label – important because oils are volatile and don't last for ever.

If you find a range of oils that are all the same price, don't buy them because the cost of producing, say, rose oil is much higher than producing rosemary or lavender. Oils should not be 'oily' – a drop on a tissue should not leave a greasy mark once it has dried.

Since pure essential oils are very expensive, they need to be stored with care to make them last. Ideally, if they are kept in amber glass jars rather than blue glass (as blue light makes them deteriorate more quickly), in a dark cool place and are tightly stoppered, they can last up to five years. Perhaps three years is more realistic after they have been opened and air enters the bottle. Once the oil has been blended with a carrier oil for massage, it will only last three to six months but, for most benefit, blend the oils only as you need them.

Carrier oils – the base into which essential oils are mixed for massage – should be either nut or seed oils, such as sweet almond oil, apricot kernel oil or grapeseed oil. Mineral oils such as baby oils have molecules that are too large to penetrate the skin. For pregnant women, grapeseed oil is recommended, as there is a slight possibility that nut oils might cause nut sensitivity in babies.

HOW SCENT WORKS

As you breathe in, the scent molecules in the air are picked up by the cilia – hair-like receptors – in the nasal mucous membrane. Scent molecules are different shapes – the mint family, for instance, has wedge-shaped molecules – and the cilia have receptors into which that particular shape will fit. These stimulate the olfactory bulbs, which then relay a message via the olfactory tract directly into the part of the brain that deals with smell, located in the area known as the limbic system. Although there is still some uncertainty about its precise function, it seems to be the pleasure centre of the brain, and the area that deals with emotional responses. In turn it stimulates the hypothalamus, which affects the pituitary gland, which influences our autonomic nervous and hormonal systems – responsible for our blood pressure, pulse rate, respiration and response to stress.

It also triggers the production of neuro-chemicals such as encephalins and endorphins, the body's own natural painkillers, and serotonin, which is a naturally produced sedative – the body's own Prozac or happy drug if you like – and, as scientists are discovering, vital for the proper functioning of many systems within the body.

Different oils trigger different responses. Rosemary, for instance, stimulates the more active beta brainwaves – good for anyone about to sit an exam – while a sweet essence such as chamomile triggers more relaxed alpha, theta and delta brainwaves. Some oils, including geranium and lavender, are balancing oils and can work either way, stimulating or relaxing depending on the individual's needs.

The area of the brain largely responsible for memory, the hippocampus, is also located within the limbic system, which is why smell is such a potent and immediate trigger for memory.

Aromatherapist Barbara Payne has worked with patients suffering from Alzheimer's disease. She reports that while none of them could remember initially

Lavender (right and below) has a powerful relaxing effect and can be as successful as some sleeping tablets in inducing restful sleep.

that they had eaten curry for lunch the previous day, after they had been given the curry plant (*Helichrysum angustifolium*) to smell, most of them did remember.

At the same time as the olfactory nerves are being stimulated, the scent molecules themselves are being drawn down into the lungs, passing through into the bloodstream and being circulated around the body to various organs and muscles where they work in various ways – analgesic, anti-inflammatory, antispasmodic and so on. Peppermint oil, for example, is now used by some surgeons in operations on the large bowel for its antispasmodic properties. Injected directly into the wall of the bowel, it prevents it from going into spasm, and so allows the surgeon to operate much more easily. When oils are used in massage, the molecules pass through the skin and into the bloodstream within twenty to ninety minutes depending on the oil, and are carried round the body in the same way.

SCIENTIFIC TRIALS

In a study carried out at Southampton General Hospital in the late 1990s, nurses who suffered from insomnia took part in a properly controlled clinical trial involving vaporized lavender oil (*Lavandula angustifolia*) for seven nights. Those taking part were not only asked to complete a questionnaire every morning, giving a subjective assessment of how they felt they had slept, but were also monitored overnight by an EEG (electroencephalogram) to monitor brain activity, and an EMG (electro-oculogram) to measure eye movement for an objective assessment.

The study showed a significant improvement in the amount and quality of sleep the nurses felt they had had, and though there were some technical problems with the EEG measurements, the objective data that was collected backed this up.

An earlier study published in *The Lancet* in 1995 found that with some geriatric patients, lavender oil was just as effective in helping them sleep as the sleeping tablets they had been previously been prescribed. Aromatherapist Barbara Payne, working with Alzheimer's patients under the supervision of a GP, was able to get a number of them off Tamezepam, a potentially addictive sleeping drug, within a couple of weeks by massaging their hands with lavender oil at night, putting a few drops on their pillow and giving them a glass of sherry. While the sherry undoubtedly helped, by itself it would not have had the same effect.

It seems that linalyl acetate and linalool are chemicals in lavender oil responsible for relaxation and are the equivalent of a light sedative. To show that it is not a placebo effect, a study carried out on mice showed that 78 per cent of those exposed to vaporized lavender oil showed a marked

decrease in mobility, while those in the control group showed no decrease in mobility whatsoever. Linalool on its own produced a 73 per cent decrease, and linalyl acetate a 69 per cent decrease.

Lavender was one of the oils used in another large-scale study, this time involving women in labour. Between 1990 and 1998 in the maternity unit at the John Radcliffe Hospital in Oxford, around 8000 pregnant women took part in the trial conducted by the Oxford Centre for Health Care Research and Development, based at Oxford Brookes University, on the use of aromatherapy in labour. A number of oils were used as well as lavender, such as chamomile, peppermint, lemon, jasmine, eucalyptus and frankincense. They were used for different reasons. One of the most important was to calm anxiety and relieve stress and tension – feelings that can affect the physical progress of labour quite considerably. Peppermint was used to help control nausea and vomiting, and for headaches in some patients, though for patients and midwives with allergies such as asthma or hay fever, it was avoided since it can cause headaches and nausea. Clary sage (*Salvia sclarea*) was used to assist contractions – an oil to be avoided during the earlier stages of pregnancy for that reason.

Sometimes the oils were used singly but at other times two or three were combined together. Clary sage, for example, has a smell that some people find unpleasant, so rose or jasmine was used with it. Peppermint, lavender and chamomile were used together in a compress for headaches while eucalyptus and lemon make a more effective remedy for a blocked nose than either one used on its own.

The oils were applied in different ways. A few drops were added to the water in the birthing pool with a teaspoonful of milk to help the oils disperse evenly, or to the water in footbaths. Diluted in carrier oil, they were used for massaging the feet, legs, back, shoulders or even the lower abdomen. Compresses – a flannel dipped in a bowl of warm or cold water with a few drops of oil added – were also used. Most oils are too strong to be used neat, but a few that are safe were applied directly – a drop of lavender or peppermint on each temple for headaches, or one of frankincense on the palm for anxiety or hyperventilation.

Although the study did not have a control group, the findings are very positive. Both patients and midwives felt that aromatherapy was very helpful during labour and childbirth, and the evidence collected shows that the percentage of women who needed such drugs as pethidine for pain relief fell from 6 per cent in 1991 to 0.4 per cent in 1997.

It could be that the release of endorphins (the body's natural painkillers) caused by scent molecules means that women need fewer pain-killing drugs.

Even so, the understanding of how smell affects us is still far from complete. As Lewis Thomas wrote in 1995, 'I should think we might fairly gauge the future of biological science, centuries ahead, by estimating the time it will take to reach a complete, comprehensive understanding of odour. It may not seem a profound enough problem to dominate all the life sciences, but it contains, piece by piece, all the mysteries.'

HOW TO USE ESSENTIAL OILS

You can use essential oils at home in many of the ways mentioned above, and there are many different ways of releasing oils into the air. You can make up a pump-action spray bottle with your chosen oil or blend of oils diluted in water, which you simply shake up and then spray into the air. Or they can be vaporized by heating either on simple ceramic burners using small tea candles, ceramic devices for attaching to radiators or circular ceramic rings with a groove for the oils, which sit on top of a light bulb. There are more elaborate electric vaporizers, which are obviously the only safe option if the oils are to be released at night – eucalyptus, for example, as a decongestant for someone with a cold.

AROMATHERAPY FROM YOUR GARDEN

While most essential oils are extracted by distillation – not a process for the amateur – you can make a milder version of, for example, rose oil, by collecting petals from a particularly fragrant rose in your garden, putting them in a clean glass jar and covering them with a carrier oil such as sweet almond or grapeseed. Leave them for a week or so and then strain the oil through muslin into a clean jar. It will be nowhere near as potent as a distilled essential oil, although of course that has to be greatly diluted for use, so an oil made in this way will still contain enough scent molecules to be beneficial in massage.

Tisanes – teas – are another easy way of using plants from your garden, but they are covered in more detail in Chapter 2, about medicinal herbs.

By careful planning you can have scent in your garden virtually all year round. Evergreen *Clematis armandii* flowers in late winter/ early spring.

Bath bags are another good way of getting the benefits of essential oils from your garden. You need a simple cotton bag about 15 × 10cm (6 × 4in), with a drawstring round the top, although you can simply tie it with twine or wool if you like. Put in a handful of your chosen herb – rosemary to stimulate you, lavender or chamomile if you want to relax – into the bag and hang it under the taps while your bath is running. Obviously you could just hang a bunch of herbs directly under the tap, but then you would get lots of bits in the water.

If you suffer from a skin condition such as eczema, try adding a couple of tablespoons of porridge oats to the herbs in the bag since they help soothe irritation. Oats and chamomile are mild enough even for a baby's skin and chamomile has the added bonus of helping the baby to sleep. Incidentally, for a baby's bath you could always use a couple of chamomile teabags if it isn't possible or convenient to use fresh.

AROMATHERAPY IN THE HEALING GARDEN

We chose scented plants for our garden to suit different moods in different areas, and of course to work in a practical way as well. For example, most of the herbs are growing in our small herb bed between the back door and the deck. This means that not only can you pick the herbs for cooking all year round without getting your feet muddy, but also that you benefit from the fragrance of the herbs when you're sitting on the deck. We planted thyme, sage, parsley, chamomile, fennel and, for drama, angelica. On chilly evenings when the chimenea is alight, add a sprig of thyme or tarragon to the burning wood, or later in the season, angelica seeds to scent the air.

Rosemary is a stimulating scent, so plant it near areas of activity.

Mint, which is always best grown by itself since it is such a garden thug, was planted in a small bed right by the back door for ease of picking. The scent is a stimulating one – good under the kitchen window – and it also helps repel insects.

In the raised beds at either end of the pool there is prostrate rosemary (*Rosmarinus prostratus*) spilling over the edges. Rosemary is also a stimulating scent, and so a good choice around the deck, which is the more active area of the garden. Between the deck and the quieter contemplative area of the garden, we planted a hedge of lavender (*L.* 'Hidcote') – a good choice because it is a balancing scent, which will relax you if you want to unwind alone but can also be an energizing fragrance if you want to enjoy the company of friends. It's also good for repelling insects – useful around an eating area.

We planted only one rose, *R.* 'Madame Isaac Pereire', with deep magenta flowers that give off one of the most powerful of all rose scents, making it a good choice to make rose oil by steeping petals in grapeseed or sweet almond oil.

We also chose a number of other scented plants which are not known to have specific therapeutic effects, other than to stimulate the limbic centre in the brain and trigger the release of the body's own 'feel good' neuro-chemicals.

For winter scent, we planted *Mahonia* × *media* 'Winter Sun', a smaller variety than 'Charity' but with similar flowers and lily-of-the-valley scent. We also planted an evergreen clematis – the fern-leafed *C. cirrhosa* var. *balearica*, with creamy bell-shaped flowers that have a faint lemon scent in winter. For spring, we planted another evergreen climber on the fences – *Holboellia latifolia*, which has greenish-white flowers in spring with a delicious sweet fragrance. To follow on in summer – honeysuckle. In our sheltered garden, we chose one of the marginally tender evergreen varieties, *Lonicera splendida*, with very fragrant flowers that are yellow on the outside and red on the inside. Among the best scented climbers for autumn are two clematis: *C. rehderiana*, the small clear primrose yellow bells of which release a delicious primrose scent – appropriately enough – and *C. flammula*, which is

smothered in small, starry, creamy white flowers at this time of year with a sweet almond scent.

CHOOSING SCENTED PLANTS FOR YOUR GARDEN

Some of the plants used in aromatherapy are very easily grown in the garden but, given the beneficial effects of fragrance in general, it is well worth growing other scented plants too.

While obviously it's possible to add scented plants to your garden at any time, to get the maximum benefit you ideally need to take it into account in the planning stage. That's because to enjoy fragrance at its best, you need a sheltered spot. While a gentle breeze will waft the fragrance through the air, stronger winds will disperse it too quickly. So, if your garden is rather exposed, you may need to

The glorious *Cosmos atrosanguineus* smells powerfully of chocolate – a healthy substitute for the real thing?

create some shelter. It's also true that many plants need warmth to release the scent fully from their flowers and foliage into the air, and shelter, particularly from a wall that can act as a storage heater, helps provide that warmth. While it would be hugely expensive to wall a whole garden, it might be possible to build a little sun trap – ideally paved since paving, too, will also store up heat and release it once the day starts to cool down. It would be the perfect place for a seat.

Create pergolas and arbours for scented plants such as roses, honeysuckle and jasmine so that you can enjoy them at nose-height. Some plants with a delicate fragrance, such as *Iris reticulata* and some daphnes, are best grown in a raised bed so that you can enjoy it without having to lie flat on the ground. Don't forget window-boxes or pots by the door – a good way to raise the scent up, and have it wafted indoors into the house.

Plants with scented foliage – rosemary, thyme, mint, lemon balm – should be planted where you can brush against them, pick the odd leaf or two, or even walk on them, releasing their fragrance into the air. Have them next to a seating area where you can rub or even pick the leaves, by a path where you might brush against them, or even in the path. Thyme and chamomile don't mind being trodden on now and again.

Although it may seem like stating the obvious, it's very important to choose fragrances that you like! For some people the rich exotic scent of regal lilies is delightful, while for others it is overpowering and gives them a headache. Some people find candytuft (*Iberis sempervirens*) has a pleasant smell, but to my colleague Stephen Lacey it smells of old stale socks!

Describing scent is even harder than describing colour and we can only compare it to other smells – hence the wilder

excesses of the 'old gymshoe with a touch of burning rubber overlaid with turpentine' school of wine expert! We talk of vanilla or almond scents – *Clematis armandii* for example, or *Sarcococca* var. *humilis*; fruity scents – of pineapple in the pineapple broom (*Cytisus battandieri*), of apples in roses such as 'Max Graf' or blackcurrant sage, or of honey scents as in the aptly named *Euphorbia mellifera* (*mellifera* means 'honey-bearing') or the giant *Crambe cordifolia*. It's a subjective way of categorizing scents, but well worth doing for yourself so that in the way you plan for colour in the garden, you can also plan for scent, with fragrances that complement each other rather than fight or cancel each other out, and create different moods in different areas.

Left: A border to please the nose, as well as the eye.

Sweet scented mock orange blossom (*Philadelphus*).

Members of the same group (see page 112) work well together – 'florals' such as roses (though there are many different rose scents) with jasmine or lavender, or 'greens' such as chamomile and thyme. In a more subjective grouping, fruity scents, like the lemon-scented *Magnolia grandiflora* or *Primula florindae*, pineapple broom, blend well with honey scents, while the heady sweet ones marry well with dry spicy clove scents from pinks, phlox and shrubs such as *Viburnum carlesii*.

Alternatively you can use just one plant en masse for an intense sensory experience – a lavender hedge, for example, a thyme pavement or a chamomile seat.

You need to take into account the seasons, too, for the comparatively few fragrances of winter are even more welcome than the positive bouquet of summer scents. Shrubs such as winter honeysuckle (*Lonicera fragrantissima*) and wintersweet (*Chimonanthus praecox*) do have a delicious scent in the depths of winter, but they quickly become very large shrubs and are of little interest in the garden once flowering is over. So rather than follow the advice to plant them in a prominent place by the front door or next to a path to enjoy their perfume, I think it's best to plant them in an out-of-the-way corner, then cut a few twigs to bring indoors and enjoy the

fragrance in the warm. A shrub such as *Sarcococca*, which has glossy evergreen leaves and delicious vanilla-scented flowers, is small and neat and worth considering by a path or door, or you could grow it in a pot in a prominent place in winter and move it to somewhere less prominent for the rest of the year.

In spring, the number of scented plants increases. There are the *burkwoodiis* – *Daphne × burkwoodii* 'Somerset' and *Viburnum × burkwoodii*, both of which have delicious sweet fragrance with a hint of clove, though perhaps *V. carlesii* has an even better scent. *Osmanthus × burkwoodii* has a strong, sweet honey/vanilla scent. The yellow azalea *Rhododendron luteum* has a powerful fruity scent, reminiscent of honeysuckle, and some of the Ghent hybrids such as 'Narcissiflorum' and 'Nancy Waterer' are also well worth growing in a fragrant garden.

In summer of course you are spoilt for choice – hundreds of roses, honeysuckle, jasmine, stocks, phlox, philadelphus, lilies … the list goes on and on.

For autumn, the list is shorter. The late Dutch honeysuckle (*Lonicera periclymenum*) carries on flowering well into October, as do some roses, but with cooler weather the scent they produce is not as strong. One of the autumn fragrance high-

Choose plants for a succession of fragrance – hyacinths in March/April, lily-of-the-valley (*Convallaria*) in May and a rose such as *Rosa* 'Ispahan' from June onwards.

lights is the katsura tree (*Cercidiphyllum japonicum*), whose fallen leaves smell distinctly of burnt sugar, but it eventually makes a large tree – too large for most small gardens.

CHOOSING SCENT FOR MOOD

For an active area in the garden, choose revitalizing, stimulating scents such as basil, citrus, eucalyptus, fennel, some scented-leafed geraniums, peppermint, rosemary, summer jasmine and thyme. Any other scents that you choose should have a fresh smell, even a sharp quality, a

tang of citrus about them perhaps – roses such as 'Leverkusen' and 'Max Graf' for example, or lemon verbena (*Lippia citriodora*), which is not hardy everywhere but worth growing in a pot in summer and bringing into a greenhouse or cool conservatory in winter.

For a tranquil area, you want calming, relaxing or balancing scents – chamomile, clary sage, scented-leafed geraniums, hops (pillows filled with dried hops are good for inducing sleep), lavender, marjoram, and roses with a rich, heavy exotic perfume rather than a lighter, fruity one. Add to that a warm afternoon, the gentle lazy buzzing of the bees, and it'll be difficult to keep your eyes open for very l...

This border provides fragrance in the day from the white rose *Rosa* 'Iceberg' and in the evenings from sweet rocket.

Ocimum basilicum (Basil)

SCENTED PLANTS

FS = flowering season
H&S = average height and spread, given after 10 years for trees and shrubs, and after one full season for the rest
E = evergreen

Unless stated otherwise, you can assume that the plant likes a moderately fertile soil, neutral, moist but not boggy.

AROMATHERAPY

Essential oils for these plants are available, and can be used for infusions and decoctions too. (See Chapter 2, pages 53–5.)

Chamaemelum nobile (Roman chamomile)
Calming. Good as analgesic for aches and pains in joints and muscles, also for soothing skin problems. Also good for PMS and menopausal symptoms.
FS Jun–Jul. White flowers. H&S 15 × 30cm (6in × 1ft). Full sun.

Eucalyptus globulus
Stimulating. Good as antiseptic and decongestant for respiratory system. Analgesic for arthritis/rheumatism.
FS Jul–Aug. Insignificant flowers. H&S 10 × 4m (32 × 13ft). E, but grown for its leaves. Full sun. Slightly tender.

Foeniculum vulgare (Fennel)
Good as detoxifier and for digestion. Stimulates oestrogen production so very good for menopause.
Avoid using oil in pregnancy. Do not use on babies or young children.
FS Aug–Sep. Yellow flowers. H&S 1.5 × 1m (5 × 3ft). Full sun. Aniseed-scented.

Jasminum officinale (Jasmine)
Promotes optimism/lifts depression. Good for skin, for pain relief in childbirth and also an aphrodisiac.
FS Jul–Sep. White flowers. H&S 7.3 × 7.3m (24 × 24ft). Sun/light shade.

Lavandula angustifolia (Lavender)
Balancing. Good for relaxation and insomnia, relieves headaches and is antiseptic, antispasmodic, analgesic and antiviral, and aids healing.
FS Jul–Sep. Blue/mauve flowers. H&S 90 × 90cm (3 × 3ft). E. Full sun.

Melissa officinalis (Lemon balm)
Soothing/relaxing. Excellent for high blood pressure, also for allergies such as asthma and eczema, and digestion.
FS Jun–Aug. Pale yellow/white flowers. Lemon-scented leaves. H&S 60 × 40cm (2 × 1ft).

Mentha × piperita (Peppermint)
Stimulating. Good general analgesic, very good for digestive problems and cooling for headaches and skin conditions.
Do not use on babies or young children.
FS Jul–Aug. Pale mauve flowers. H&S 30 × 90cm (1 × 3ft) Full sun/part shade.

Ocimum basilicum (Basil)
Stimulating. Good for the digestive, respiratory and nervous system.
FS Aug–Sep (if protected over winter). Insignificant flowers. H&S 45 × 30cm (1ft 6in × 1ft). Treated as an annual 20 × 20cm (8 × 8in). Full sun.

Origanum majorana (Marjoram)
Comforting. Good for digestion, respiratory system, headaches and for pain of arthritis/rheumatism.
Avoid essential oil in pregnancy.
FS Jun–Sep. White flowers. H&S 60 × 60cm (2 × 2ft). Full sun.

Pelargonium odoratissimum
Balancing. Good as analgesic for arthritis/rheumatism, for skin, for varicose veins, and for the meno pause and PMT.
FS May–Jun. White flowers. H&S 20 × 30cm (8 × 12in). E. Sun/light shade. Apple-scented leaves.

Rosa* × *centifolia*/× *damascena
Calming/balancing. Good for female reproductive problems, for skin care and for constipation. FS Jun–Jul. Pink flowers. H&S 1.5 × 1.2m (5 × 4ft). Full sun.

Rosmarinus officinalis (Rosemary)
Stimulating. Good as pain relief in muscles/joints, for digestive system, respiratory system, heart, and as a diuretic.
FS May–Jun. Blue flowers. H&S 1.2 × 1.5m (4 × 5ft). E. Full sun.

Salvia officinalis (Sage)
Stimulating. Like rosemary, good for pain relief in muscles and joints, for digestive and respiratory systems, and as a diuretic. Also good for the circulation, and for some female reproductive problems. **Avoid essential oil in early pregnancy. Do not use on babies or young children.**
FS Jun–Jul. Blue flowers. H&S 1m × 60cm (3 × 2ft). E. Full sun.

Salvia sclarea (Clary sage)
Sedative. Stimulates contractions so good for childbirth.
Avoid essential oil in pregnancy.
FS Jun–Aug. Blue and white flowers. H&S 50 × 20cm (20 × 8in). Full sun.

Thymus vulgaris (Thyme)
Energizing. Good for boosting immune system, for circulation, treating problems with respiratory system, warming up stiff joints. Also good for urinary infections.
Avoid essential oil in pregnancy. Don't use on babies.
FS Jun–Aug. Mauve flowers. H&S 20 × 30cm (8 × 12in). E. Full sun.

OTHER SCENTED PLANTS

Winter
CLIMBERS
***Clematis armandii* 'Apple Blossom'**
FS Mar–Apr. White flowers. E. H&S 6 × 6m (20 × 20ft). Foliage full sun. Roots in shade.

Clematis cirrhosa* var. *balearica
FS Jan–Mar. Pale yellow flowers. E.

H&S 2.5 × 2.5m (8 × 8ft). Sun/light shade. Roots in shade.

SHRUBS
***Hamamelis* × *intermedia* 'Pallida'**
FS Jan–Feb. Yellow flowers. H&S 3 × 4m (10 × 13ft). Sun/light shade.

Iris reticulata
FS Feb. Blue flowers. H&S 10–15 × 5cm (4–6 × 2in). Full sun. Bulb.

Lonicera* × *purpusii
FS Jan–Mar. White flowers.

Iris reticulata

Semi-E. H&S 1.5 × 1.5m (5 × 5ft).
Partial shade.

Sarcococca humilis
FS Jan–Feb. White flowers.
Vanilla/almond scent. E. H&S
50 × 20cm (20 × 8in). Sun/
medium shade.

Viburnum farreri
FS Mar–Apr. White/pink flowers.
H&S 2.5 × 2m (8 × 6ft). Sun/
medium shade.

Spring
CLIMBERS
Clematis montana var. wilsonii
FS Mar–Apr. White flowers. H&S
9 × 9m (30 × 30ft). Sun/medium
shade. Roots in shade.

Holboellia latifolia
FS Apr–May. Cream flowers. E.
H&S 6 × 3m (20 × 10ft). Sun/par-
tial shade. Not hardy in colder sites.

FLOWERS
Convallaria majalis (Lily-of-the-
valley)
FS Apr–May. White flowers. H&S
15 × 45cm (6 × 18in). Light shade.

SHRUBS
Corylopsis pauciflora
FS Mar–May. Yellow flowers. H&S
1.2 –2 × 1.2 –2m (4–6 × 4–6ft).
Neutral to acid, moist, well-
drained soil. Light/medium shade.

Daphne × burkwoodii
FS Apr–May. Pink/white flowers,
lily-scented. H&S 80 × 70cm
(2ft 8in × 2ft 4in). Neutral to acid,
moist, well-drained soil. Light
shade.

Rhododendron Ghent Hybrids
FS May–Jun. Flowers range from
white, yellow, pink, to orange and
red. H&S 1.5–2.4m × 1.5–2.4m
(5–8 × 5–8ft). Acid soil. Light
shade.

Rhododendron luteum
FS May–Jun. Yellow flowers. H&S
1.5–2.4m × 1.5–2.4m (5–8 × 5–8ft).
Acid soil. Light shade.

Syringa microphylla 'Superba'
FS Apr–May. Pale mauve flowers.
H&S 80 × 80cm (2ft 6in × 2ft
6in). Sun/light shade.

Viburnum × bodnantense
FS Mar–Apr. White/pink flowers.
H&S 2.5 × 2m (8 × 6ft). Sun/
medium shade.

Viburnum carlesii
FS Apr–May. White/pink flowers.
H&S 1.5 × 1.5m (5 × 5ft). Light
shade.

Lonicera × purpusii

Summer

CLIMBERS

Lathyrus odoratus (Sweet pea)
FS Jun–Sep. Various coloured
flowers. H&S 2m × 30cm (6 × 1ft).
Full sun.

Lonicera japonica 'Halliana'
(Japanese honeysuckle)
FS Jun–Jul. Yellow and white flow-
ers. E. H&S 4.9 × 4.9m (16 × 16ft).
Light shade.

Rosa 'Alister Stella Gray'
FS Jul–Aug. Yellow flowers, ageing
to white. H&S 4.6 × 4.6m
(15 × 15ft). Full sun.

Rosa 'Constance Spry'
FS Jul–Aug. Rich pink flowers.
H&S 6 × 3.7m (20 × 12ft). Sun/
light shade.

Rosa 'Guinée'
FS Jun–Aug. Dark red flowers.
H&S 4.6 × 4.6m (15 × 15ft). Sun/
medium shade.

Rosa 'Leverkusen'
FS Jun–Sep. Lemon-yellow
flowers, lemon scent. H&S 4.6 ×
4.6m (15 × 15ft). Sun/medium
shade.

Trachelospermum asiaticum
FS Jul–Aug. Cream flowers. E.
H&S 3.7 × 3.7m (12 × 12ft). Sun/
light shade.

FLOWERS

Lilium 'Pink Perfection' Group
FS Jun–Jul. Pink flowers. H&S
90cm–1.5m × 25cm (3–5ft × 10in).
Sun/light shade.

Lilium regale
FS Jun–Jul. White flowers. H&S
90cm–1.5m × 25cm (3–5ft × 10in).
Sun/light shade.

Matthiola White Perennial stocks
FS Jul–Aug. White flowers. H&S
60 × 50cm (2 × 1ft). Full sun.

Nicotiana sylvestris (tobacco
plant)
FS Jun–Aug. White flowers. H&S
1.5m × 45cm (5ft × 18in). Sun/part
shade.

Oenothera biennis (evening
primrose)
FS Jun–Aug. Yellow flowers. H&S
1.2m × 60cm (4 × 2ft). Full sun.

ROSES

Rosa 'Graham Thomas'
FS Jul–Sep. Egg-yolk yellow
flowers. H&S 1.2 × 1.5m (4 × 5ft).
Sun/light shade.

Rosa 'Ispahan'
FS Jun–Aug. Pink flowers. H&S
2.1 × 2.1m (7 × 7ft). Sun/light
shade.

Rosa 'Madame Hardy'
FS Jul–Aug. White flowers. H&S
1.5 × 1.2m (5 × 4ft). Sun/light
shade.

Rosa 'Max Graf' (Ground cover)
FS Jun–Sep. Silver-pink flowers.
H&S 60cm × 1.2m (2 × 4ft)
Sun/light shade.

SHRUBS

Buddleia fallowiana var. alba
(butterfly bush)
FS Aug–Sep. White flowers. H&S
2 × 2m (6 × 6ft). Full sun.

Cistus × purpureus
FS May–Aug. Magenta flowers. E.
H&S 1.5 × 1m (5 × 3ft). Full sun.

Euphorbia mellifera
FS Apr–May. Tan flowers, honey
scent. E. H&S 2 × 2m (6 × 6ft).
Full sun.

Genista aetnensis (Mount Etna
broom)
FS May–Jun. Yellow flowers. H&S
3.5 × 3.5m (12 × 12ft). Full sun.

**Philadelphus 'Manteau
d'Hermine'**
FS Jul–Aug. White flowers. H&S
1 × 1m (3 × 3ft). Sun/medium shade.

Philadelphus 'Virginal'
FS Jun–Jul. White flowers. H&S
2.5 × 2m (8 × 6ft). Sun/medium
shade.

Autumn

CLIMBERS

Lonicera periclymenum 'Serotina'
FS Jul–Oct. White/yellow flowers.
H&S 3.7 × 3.7m (12 × 12ft). Light/
medium shade.

SHRUBS

Rosa 'Souvenir de la Malmaison'
FS Jun–Sep. Pale pink flowers.
H&S 1.5 × 1.5m (5 × 5ft). Sun/light
shade.

TREES

Cercidiphyllum japonicum
(katsura tree)
Its leaves in autumn smell strongly
of burnt toffee. H&S 7 × 5m (24 ×
17ft) Rich, moist but well-drained
acid to neutral soil. Sun/part shade.

FLOWER REMEDIES

It is not only the fragrance of flowers that can be beneficial to us. Remedies made from the flowers themselves can also be used to treat various health problems, and while not so long ago such treatments were considered somewhat cranky, it's a sign of the times that you can now buy flower remedies at most high street chemists.

The most famous flower remedies are the Bach Flower remedies, created by Dr Edward Bach – pronounced 'Batch' incidentally, not as in the composer – in the 1920s and 30s. Dr Bach was an eminent London physician, pathologist

Mount Vernon, near Wallingford in Oxford-shire, was the home of Dr Edward Bach. It is now the Bach Centre and many of the plants used in his flower reme-dies are still grown in the garden.

and bacteriologist who, through his work, became disillusioned with what Stefan Ball, co-principal of the Bach Centre in Oxfordshire, calls the 'car mechanic' approach of orthodox medicine to disease – dealing with illness symptom by symptom rather than looking at the whole person. He believed, long before the days of psychoneuroimmunology, that negative emotions such as unhappiness, fear, anxiety or guilt were at the source of many illnesses, and that the way forward was to treat the whole patient through his or her emotions. This way, he felt, many illnesses could be prevented, and if they did develop the patient could be helped to overcome them more quickly.

In 1917, he had first-hand experience of the power of positive thought. Having had a cancerous growth removed, he was told by his doctors that he had only a matter of months to live. But he was so determined to pursue his work that he was back in his laboratory as soon as he could stand up, and in fact lived for another eighteen years. He had been able to overcome a potentially fatal illness, he believed, because he had a purpose in life. This convinced him that if other people who were ill could be given back their sense of purpose, and helped to overcome apathy and hopelessness, they, too, could recover. As he said, it is 'our fears, our cares, our anxieties and such like that open the path to the invasion of illness'.

Early on in his medical career Dr Bach studied homeopathy at the London Homeopathic Hospital, from which he learnt two valuable lessons. The first was the idea of 'type' remedies, which treat the personality rather than the symptoms, and the second, the idea that minute doses of a substance – so minute that they do not appear in any chemical analysis – are very effective. Although he worked initially on creating vaccines to treat chronic bowel

diseases from bacteria found in the gut of people suffering from those diseases, he wanted to find treatments that treated the person rather than the symptoms, and that were as pure and natural as possible – and plants seemed the obvious source.

In 1928, he set out to find seven plants to replace the seven vaccines he had developed and found his first three plant remedies – the monkey flower (*Mimulus guttatus*), old man's beard (*Clematis vitalba*) and a form of *Impatiens*, Himalayan balsam (*Impatiens glandulifera*). He prepared them using the same homeopathic techniques in a laboratory as he had used to make the vaccines. Initially he used them to treat the same group of patients as he had treated with vaccines, but soon realized the flower remedies worked in a different way – on the emotions – and therefore they could be used on a much wider range of patients and for a whole range of diseases.

Dr Bach found that *Mimulus*, for example, was a remedy for people who had a fear of or anxiety about something specific – the dark, speaking to a large group of people, spiders and so forth. *Clematis* was good for people who daydreamed but did nothing to make their dreams a reality, while *Impatiens*, as its name suggests, was a good remedy for people who lived life in a rush and put themselves under unnecessary pressure.

Excited by his discovery, he gave up his medical career in London in 1930 and over the next four years walked extensively through the southern half of England looking for more flower remedies. By the time he settled down again, at a small cottage called Mount Vernon, near Wallingford in Oxfordshire, which is still home to the Dr Edward Bach Centre, he had discovered another thirty-five remedies, making a total of thirty-eight altogether. One remedy is 'rock water', which is water taken from a pure spring and prepared by the sun method (see page 139). Apart from *Ceratostigma willmottianum*, the remaining thirty-six were all plants that grow wild in the British Isles.

There are now Bach practitioners in thirty-five different countries around the world, and over the years other people have explored the potential of their own native flora for new flower remedies. In California, for example, in the 1970s around ninety different remedies were developed – some very 1970s California, such as alpine lily for women who idealize femininity in an abstract way but find it hard to accept their physicality and sexuality, or chapparal (*Larrea tridentata*) for those whose psyches are overburdened by an excess of violent images from city life and the media.

In Australia a naturopath, Ian White, who had used Bach flower remedies, developed and researched a range of over sixty new ones from the native Australian flora, called Bush Flower Essences.

Bach practitioners stick to the good doctor's original thirty-eight, and while that may seem a very small number of remedies to cover the whole complicated range of human emotions, in fact they can be blended together to give almost 293 million possible combinations – enough to cover any emotional state that might arise no matter how complex. In all the years the Bach Centre has been in operation, practitioners have never had to say to a client, 'Sorry, we have nothing that can help you.'

Some remedies treat personality types – daydreamers, people who are always critical of others, those who lack confidence in themselves and assume they will fail at whatever they try – and others treat emotional states – depression following a setback, shock, mental exhaustion. Some remedies can treat both.

Although Edward Bach had trained as a doctor at a time when doctors really were gods, he was also most unusual in that he wanted his flower remedies to be a self-help therapy. He saw the role of the practitioner as not simply prescribing treatment but teaching patients how to decide on the remedies for themselves and also how to prepare them in their own homes.

Taking a remedy ought to be, he said,

Sweet chestnut (*Castanea sativa*) for people in total dispair.

as simple and obvious as eating a lettuce when we are hungry. That, Stefan Ball believes, is one reason why the flower remedies have become so popular over the last ten or fifteen years. Not only are people turning to natural alternatives to drugs, but they want to take more responsibility for their own health.

Dr Bach believed that remedies should be part of everyday life, something we take when we feel out of sorts, unhappy or not quite ourselves, rather than waiting until that sense of dis-ease turns into full-blown illness.

Remedies can be taken singly or in combination. Stefan Ball cites the case of a woman whose daughter finally became pregnant after years of trying and several attempts at IVF. She came to stay and virtually took over, refusing to let her daughter do anything. Finally the daughter's irritation erupted and her mother revealed for the first time that she had suffered late miscarriage before her daughter was born and was afraid that the same thing might happen to the daughter.

The treatment recommended was red chestnut (*Aesculus × carnea*), the remedy for people who worry about others to such an extent that the latter's confidence is undermined. Star of Bethlehem (*Ornithogalum umbellatum*), a remedy for shock and grief, was also recommended because although the miscarriage had happened a very long time ago, it seemed as though the mother had never fully come to terms with it. Agrimony (*Agrimonia eupatoria*) might have helped her talk about what had happened in the past and her feelings about it rather than hiding it, while centaury (*Centaurium umbellatum*) might have helped the daughter feel strong enough to stand up for what she wanted earlier.

Bach practitioners always start by treating how the person feels at the moment, and when that feeling has resolved either

Agrimony (*Agrimonia eupatoria*) for those who find it hard to share their problems.

stop the treatment altogether or, if other negative emotions have been revealed, find a new remedy for the way he/she is feeling now. They call the process 'peeling the onion'. In another case study a woman consulted a Bach practitioner because of recurrent cystitis. The consultation revealed her to be impatient and irritable with colleagues at work, and inclined to be a bit of a bully to get things done as she wanted. She was prescribed impatiens and vine, the remedy for people who are strong and decisive to the point of being overbearing, for three weeks. At her next consultation, she felt she was a little less impatient, but for the first time revealed that her only son had died four years earlier. She was then given Star of Bethlehem to help her overcome the shock and grief she had felt but had never properly dealt with. At the same time she was given honeysuckle to help her focus on the present. Her cystitis disappeared and six months later had not recurred.

While you can mix remedies together for your own needs – six or seven is the usually recommended limit – the only ready-mixed remedy on sale is the famous Rescue Remedy. This contains rock rose (*Helianthemum nummularium*) for terror and extreme fear, clematis for the disconnected feelings that can happen in an emergency, Star of Bethlehem for shock and grief, impatiens to calm the feelings of agitation, and cherry plum (*Prunus cerasifera*) to promote rational thought and prevent irrational behaviour. In 1960 a colleague of Dr Bach's, Nora Weeks created Rescue Cream, for external injuries, based on Rescue Remedy with the addition of crab apple as a cleanser. Although the cream contains natural healers such as honey, it still works on the same basis – treating the emotional imbalances caused

Water violets (*Hottonia palustris*), a remedy for people who are so self-contained that they can become very lonely.

by the injury rather than the injury itself. It's just that the remedies are absorbed through the skin rather than via the digestive system.

How flower remedies work

The short answer here is that nobody knows how flower remedies work. Certainly, there is no chemistry involved since analysis of the flower remedies shows only the constituents of water and brandy. When Dr Bach was working on his remedies he talked in terms of vibrations of the plant's life force captured in the potentized water and there are some Kirlian photographs (see pages 88–9) which show distinctly different patterns produced by different remedies. These days, some people also talk in terms of new theories in quantum physics which suggests that all forms of existence, whether it's Mount Everest or a brain wave, are all simply energy vibrating at different frequencies – the former imperceptibly slowly, the latter almost imperceptibly fast. The vibration of the plant's energy, they suggest, could correspond with and subtly alter a particular frequency in the patient. And there's the fact that we share 35 per cent of our genes with plants.

Some research has been done into the effects of flower remedies. In California in the 1970s one study found that the group taking four remedies achieved a significantly higher degree of self-acceptance and understanding than those taking the placebo. More recent work in Italy shows positive results, too. One study done over three years on children between birth and fourteen showed the remedies were very effective in dealing with emotional problems. Another study by two Italian doctors, D'Auria and Pezza, showed that some remedies have a marked effect on crystalline minerals called phyllosilicates which are found in soil and are a factor in some lung diseases. Having proved definitively that the Bach flower remedies do have an effect on inorganic substances, they say the next stage is to try and devise a way of measuring the impact on organic, living substances.

While Bach practitioners are very interested in any research being done, they do not feel the need for scientific validation and certainly would not dress up their work in pseudo-science. What concerns them is that the patient gets better, not how the patient gets better. Nor are they concerned if people put any successes the treatments have down to a placebo effect. As has already been stated, the power of the mind to affect physical health is becoming increasingly widely accepted in all fields of medicine. What's more, practitioners know from the success the remedies have in situations where a placebo effect isn't an issue, with babies or animals, for example, or people who have been given the remedies without their knowledge (although they do not recommend this), that there is more to it than that.

Making flower remedies

The method of making the flower remedies is very simple, and unlike homeopathic remedies or essential oils, something you can do in your own garden. Most of the remedies are made by what's called the sun method.

You need a small, thin glass bowl, a bottle of still mineral water, a clean 30ml (1oz) bottle and some 40 per cent proof brandy. Choose a sunny day to gather the flowers, ideally early in the morning while the dew is still on the plants. First, pour the water into the bowl, then cut the flower heads with scissors so they fall into the water, until the surface is completely covered and all the flowers are still in contact with the water. Ideally take the flowers from as many different plants as you can and avoid touching them with your hands because the warmth can speed the degeneration process. If for some reason it's not possible to drop the flowers straight into the water, then place a broad leaf on your hand and cut the flowers on to that. Then stand the bowl as close to the parent plants as possible and in full sunshine to potentize the water, and leave it for at least three hours. If the sun goes in for any length of time, so that the bowl is not exposed for three hours continuously, then you should abandon the remedy. Equally, don't leave the flowers for much longer than three hours otherwise they may start to die and rot in the water, and the positive healing properties will be lost.

At the end of the time, carefully remove the flowers from the water, ideally using a twig of the same plant. Before describing the next step, I'll deal with the other method of preparation, which is used for woody plants such as beech, holly, pine and wild rose and for those that flower in early spring when the sun isn't warm enough to potentize the water. This is the boiling method.

For this, you need a large enamel or stainless steel saucepan (ideally 3.5 litre/ 6 pints), a bottle of still mineral water, two small glass or china jugs, a small glass dropper bottle, all sterilized by boiling, some filter paper and some brandy. Again, you should pick the twigs or flowers on a sunny day early in the morning. Take the saucepan with you to the site and fill it three-quarters full with flowers, twigs or young leaves. Take it back to the kitchen, and cover the plant material with 1 litre (2 pints) of still mineral water. Place the saucepan without a lid over the heat and bring it to the boil. If necessary, press the plant material under the surface of the water with a twig of the same plant. Boil it for half an hour, and then remove the saucepan from the heat and leave it until the water is cold. Remove as much of the plant material as you can with another twig of the same plant, then leave the saucepan to stand for a while to let the sediment settle as much as possible. Place the filter paper over the neck of one jug and, using the other jug to fill from the saucepan, pour the liquid a little at a time over the filter paper.

The next step is the same for both the sun method and the boiling method. Half-fill the clean bottle with the potentized water and then top up with brandy to preserve it. This is called the mother tincture and should be labelled as such. To make the stock remedy – the one you use all the time – you need just two

drops of mother tincture to 30ml (1fl oz) of brandy, only 25 per cent proof this time. This is the dilution at which you buy the Flower Remedies in the shops – two-thirds of a drop in 10ml of brandy.

You can take the remedies in several ways. First, you can add two drops of each remedy you are taking (or four of Rescue Remedy) to a glass of water and sip it at intervals. It really doesn't matter how large the glass of water is or how big a sip you take or how often. This can be difficult at first for people used to taking drugs in precise quantities and at regular intervals, but you will get the minimum dose from each sip and you can't take too much.

Another method, easier if you are taking the remedies long term, is to make up a treatment bottle. You need another 30ml dropper bottle to which you add two drops of each remedy (four of Rescue Remedy) and top up with still mineral water. You then take four drops four times a day either in liquid or, if that's not possible, directly on to your tongue. For people who have a sensitivity to alcohol, even in the minute quantities contained in the remedies, the drops can be added to a very hot drink so that the very small amount of alcohol is evaporated away.

Plants for flower remedies

Apart from *Ceratostigma willmottianum*, Dr Bach collected all the plants he used for flower remedies initially from the wild, and later established most of them in the garden of Mount Vernon, his cottage in Oxfordshire where many are still used to make mother tinctures today. These days, you should not take plants from the wild but you can grow many of them in your garden. Do make sure that you grow only the specific plants mentioned and not near-relatives. In this case the Latin name really is invaluable!

Obviously in the 1930s when Dr Bach first collected the plants, there was far less atmospheric pollution than there is now, and unless you live in the very heart of the country it's impossible to find anywhere that is completely free of pollution. Do the best you can, though. Find an area that's as far away as possible from a road or other source of pollution. Since you're trying to replicate the conditions in which the plants would have grown in the wild, grow them organically, without chemicals and without overfeeding. In the garden at Mount Vernon, the plants are virtually left to get on with it, being thinned out or pruned back as necessary.

Collecting the flowers of *Ceratostigma willmottianum* for a home-made flower remedy.

Chichorium intybus (Chicory)

THE FLOWER REMEDIES

FS = flowering season
H&S = average height and spread, given after 10 years for trees and shrubs, and after one full season for the rest
E = evergreen

Unless stated otherwise, you can assume that the plant likes a moderately fertile soil, neutral, moist but not boggy.

Aesculus × carnea (Red chestnut)
For people who worry too much about the welfare of those they care about to the extent that they undermine the confidence of the objects of their anxieties.
Prepare 15cm (6in) twigs with young leaves and flower spikes by the boiling method.
FS May–Jun. H&S 5 × 5m (16 × 16ft). Sun/light shade.

Aesculus hippocastanum (Chestnut bud)
For people who find it impossible to learn from their mistakes, and repeat them over and over. Either they don't recognize the pattern at all, or do but fail to learn effectively from experience.
Prepare 15cm (6in) twigs of sticky buds by the boiling method.
FS Apr–May. Seed ripens Sep. H&S 12 × 10m (39 × 32ft). Full sun.

Aesculus hippocastanum (White chestnut)
For people whose brains never stop working with worrying, unwanted and persistent thoughts that go round and round in circles.
Prepare the male and female flowers by the sun method.
FS May. Seed ripens Sep. H&S 12 × 10m (39 × 32ft). Full sun.

Agrimonia eupatoria (Agrimony)
For people who always put on a cheerful face, no matter bad things are and don't share their worries with other people. They are peacemakers, always keen to smooth over any conflict.
Prepare the flowers by the sun method.
FS Jun–Aug. H&S 60 × 45cm (2 × 1ft). Moist, slightly alkaline soil. Sun/light shade.

Bromus ramosus (Wild oat)
For people who have a genuine desire to do something worthwhile in life, but can't decide what it should be so they often drift and feel frustrated.
Prepare the flowering spikelets by the sun method.
FS Jul–Aug. H&S 1.5m × 15cm (5ft × 6in). Average to moist soil. Full sun.

Calluna vulgaris (Heather)
For people Dr Bach described as 'buttonholers' – very talkative people who need to be listened to because they fear loneliness. They can be so self-obsessed that they drive the listener away, bringing about the situation they dread.
Prepare young flowering shoots by the sun method.

FS Jul–Oct. H&S 40cm × 1m (15in × 3 ft). E. Moist, acidic soil. Sun/light shade.

Carpinus betulus (Hornbeam)
For people who look at all the work they have to do and are overcome with tiredness, feeling that they will not be able to get it done. It's a mental tiredness rather than a physical one.
Prepare 15cm (6in) twigs with catkins by the boiling method.
FS Apr–May (catkins). H&S 8 × 6m (26 × 20ft). Sun/medium shade.

Castanea sativa (Sweet chestnut)
For people who have reached the end of their endurance and, having explored all the options, are in total despair, unlike Gorse people who give up before exploring all avenues.
Prepare 15cm (6 in) twigs with leaves, and both male and female flowers by the boiling method.
FS Jun–Aug. Catkins Jul. Nuts Oct. H&S 14 × 6m (46 × 20ft). Any soil type. Sun/light shade.

Centaurium erythraea (Centaury)
For people who find it impossible to stand up for themselves and say no to the demands of others. They

are kind gentle people who are always willing to help, and therefore are easily exploited by the more ruthless.

Prepare the flowers by the sun method.

FS Jun–Oct. H&S 25 × 15cm (10 × 6in). Full sun.

Ceratostigma willmottianum (Hardy plumbago)

For people who don't trust their own decisions and constantly need reassurance from other people. The almost inevitably conflicting advice they receive leaves them more uncertain than before.

Prepare the flowers by the sun method.

FS Jul–Sep. H&S 1 × 1m (3 × 3ft). Full sun.

Cichorium intybus (Chicory)

For people who need to be needed. While they are loving, it is not a selfless love in that they demand to be loved in return. They can be possessive and manipulative.

Prepare the flowers by the sun method.

FS Jul–Oct. H&S 1.5m × 50cm (5 × 1ft). Full sun.

Clematis vitalba (Clematis)

For people who are daydreamers but never get round to making their dreams a reality.

Prepare the flowers by the sun method.

FS Jul–Oct. Seedheads Oct–Jan. H&S 3.7 × 3.7m (12 × 12ft). Sun/light shade.

Fagus sylvatica (Beech)

For people who are intolerant and openly critical of others whose ideas, attitudes and believes are different from theirs.

Prepare young shoots about 15cm (6in) long with flowers and young leaves by the boiling method.

FS Apr–May. H&S 8 × 8m (26 × 26ft). Any soil type. Sun/light shade.

Gentiana or Gentianella amarella (Gentian)

For people who feel discouraged by a setback or for those who are generally easily discouraged.

Prepare the flowers by the sun method.

FS Aug–Sep. H&S 15 × 8cm (6 × 3in). Chalky soil. Wild plant, difficult to cultivate. Sun/light shade.

Helianthemum nummularium (Rock rose)

For people who suffer from extreme fear, panic or terror normally of something specific, and is much stronger than mimulus fear. It's a constituent of Rescue Remedy.

Prepare the yellow flowers by the sun method.

FS Jul–Sep. H&S 50cm × 1m (1ft 8in × 3ft). E. Neutral to alkaline soil. Full sun.

Hottonia palustris (Water violet)

For quiet, self-contained people who can seem stand-offish and proud. They don't get involved in other people's problems or discuss their own with other people but can sometimes feel lonely.

Prepare the flowers by the sun method.

FS May-Jun. H up to 90cm (3ft), indefinite spread. Water plant. Full sun.

Ilex aquifolium (Holly)

For people with strong negative emotions such as envy, hatred and spitefulness and the anger associated with them.

Prepare shoots with male and female flowers by the boiling method.

Nov–Feb. H&S 4 × 2.5m (13 × 8ft). Sun/medium shade. FS May–Jun. Berries ripen

Impatiens glandulifera (Impatiens)

For people who are (not surprisingly) impatient and irritable, who live life in a rush and put unnecessary pressure on themselves by doing so.

Castanea sativa (Sweet chestnut)

Prepare by the sun method, using only the pale mauve flowers. FS Aug–Oct. H&S 1.5 × 1m (5 × 3ft). Moist soil. Partial shade.

Juglans regia (Walnut)
For people who are too easily led by the actions and opinions of other people or who cling on to old patterns of thought and behaviour.
Prepare 15cm (6in) shoots with only small, female flowers by the boiling method.
FS Apr–May. Nuts ripen Oct. H&S 8 × 3m (26 × 10ft). Any soil type. Sun/medium shade.

Larix decidua (Larch)
For people who lack confidence in themselves and assume that they are always going to fail to such an extent that they avoid taking up challenges at which they would undoubtedly succeed.
Prepare 15cm (6in) twigs with young leaf tufts and catkins by the boiling method.
FS Apr–May (catkins). Cones ripen Oct–Nov. H&S 30 × 6m (100 × 20ft). Full sun.

Lonicera caprifolium (Honeysuckle)
For people who live in the past and so escape dealing with the realities of the present. They are often nostalgic, seeing the past as the golden era that can never be equalled.
Prepare 15cm (6in) shoots with clusters of flowers and leaves by the boiling method.
FS Jul–Aug. H&S 3.5 × 3.5m (12 × 12ft). Light shade.

Malus pumila (Crab apple)
For people who are fussy – even too fussy – about cleanliness and tidiness, focusing often on small, less relevant details while missing the big picture.
Prepare spurs with leaves and flowers by the boiling method.
FS Apr. Red/purple fruit in autumn. H&S 6 × 8m (20 × 25ft). Sun/partial shade.

Mimulus guttatus (Mimulus)
For people who have fears of something specific – mice, flying, the dark – and who keep them to themselves.
Prepare the flowers by the sun method.
FS Jul–Sep. H&S 50 × 60cm (1 × 2ft). Very moist soil. Full sun.

Olea europaea (Olive)
For people suffering from complete exhaustion, physical or mental, after a great deal of effort.
Prepare the flowers by the sun method.
FS Jul–Aug. Rarely fruits in Britain. E. Full sun.

Ornithogalum umbellatum (Star of Bethlehem)
For people who have suffered shock or trauma, both at the time it happens and later if it has not been resolved. It is another ingredient of Rescue Remedy.
Prepare the fully open flower spikes by the boiling method.
FS Apr–May. H&S 20 × 10cm (8 × 4 in). Sun/part shade. Bulb.

Pinus sylvestris (Pine)
For people who reproach themselves when things go wrong,

and feel guilty even when it isn't their fault.
Prepare young 15cm (6 in) shoots with male and female flowers by the boiling method.
FS May–Jun. H&S 15 × 6m (50 × 20ft)). E. Full sun.

Populus tremula (Aspen)
For people whose fear has no obvious cause, whether it is a mild anxiety or near-terror.
Prepare both male and female catkins along with 15cm (6in) lengths of twigs and leaf buds by the boiling method.
FS Feb–Mar (catkins). H&S 4 × 2m (13 × 6ft). Full sun.

Prunus cerasifera (Cherry plum)
For people who fear they will lose control of themselves, and particularly of their temper, and harm themselves or someone else.
Prepare 15cm (6in) flowering twigs by the boiling method.
FS Feb–Mar. Dark purple fruit Aug–Sep. H&S 6 × 3m (20 × 10ft). Sun/light shade.

Quercus robur (Oak)
For people who battle on in difficult circumstances without losing hope, but who can also fail to realize when the battle is lost.
Prepare only the tiny female flowers (not the male catkin-like flowers), by the sun method.
FS Apr–May. Acorns ripen Sep–Oct. H&S 7 × 5m (23 × 16ft). Sun/light shade.

Rosa canina (Wild rose)
For people who are happy-go-lucky, but can easily drift into passivity, apathy or resignation.

Prepare the flowers, leaves and short pieces of stem by the boiling method.
FS Jun–Jul. H&S 3 × 3m (10 × 10ft). Sun/part shade.

Salix alba subsp. *vitellina* (Willow)

For people who are self-pitying, resentful and bitter, blaming other people for their misfortune.
Prepare 15cm (6in) twigs with catkins of both sexes, and young leaves, by the boiling method.
FS Apr–May (catkins). H&S 8 × 3.5m (26 × 12ft). Sun/medium shade.

Scleranthus annuus (Scleranthus)

For people who are indecisive and can't choose between positive, known options.
Prepare the flowers by the sun method.

FS Jun–Aug. H&S 10 × 10cm (4 × 4in). Well-drained acidic soil.

Sinapis arvensis (Mustard)

For people who suffer from deep depression and hopelessness for which there is no external cause.
Prepare the flower heads by the boiling method.
FS May–Jul. H&S 75 × 25cm (2ft × 10in). Full sun.

Ulex europaeus (Gorse)

For people who have given up hope as the result of something that has happened in their lives and are convinced that nothing can make things better. They don't enjoy their misery, though.
Prepare the flowers by the sun method.
FS Apr–May (intermittently throughout the year). E. H&S 1.5 × 1.5m (5 × 5ft). Full sun.

Ulmus procera (Elm)

For people who have great faith in their own abilities, so often take on too much and then find the weight of responsibility too much to bear.
Prepare 15cm (6in) flowering twigs by the boiling method.
FS Feb–Mar. H&S 6 × 4m (20 × 13ft). Sun/light shade.

Verbena officinalis (Vervain)

For people whose enthusiasm for a project or a cause can turn to fanaticism, determined to win other people over to their own beliefs without listening to other points of view.
Prepare the youngest open flowering spikes by the sun method.
FS Jul–Sep. H&S 60 × 50cm (2ft × 1ft 8in). Full sun.

Vitis vinifera (Vine)

For strong-minded people who are inclined to be ruthless and impose their will on other people. They can be leaders or bullies.
Prepare the flowering clusters at their peak by the sun method.
FS May–Jun. Fruit ripe Sep–Oct. H&S 5.5 × 5.5m (18 × 18ft). Any soil type. Sun/medium shade.

Rock water

Still called a flower remedy though it contains no flowers, this is for people who are too hard on themselves and set impossibly high standards.
Prepare by taking water from a natural spring, and leaving it in the sun for three hours ideally in June, July or August.

Verbena officinalis (Vervain)

Water, water, everywhere..

Water is hugely important to human beings and we have a great affinity with it. It's the medium from which life on Earth evolved, it's a precondition for all life and it still covers seven-eighths of our planet. What's more, we start our lives in water – in amniotic fluid – and it makes up over 70 per cent of our bodies. While we can survive without food for weeks, without water we die within days. Water is endlessly renewable energy. Think of the power of an angry sea or a river in full spate. Even in its smallest form – a drop – it can eventually wear its way right through the hardest rock. Water is eternal, ever-changing, yet always the same.

Fast-moving water is exciting, exhilarating and makes us feel better in body and spirit.

It has a fascination for us that starts with the inability to see a puddle without jumping in it when we are two and stays with us all our lives. Whenever there is water nearby – whether it's the sea, a stream or even a tiny barrel pond on a patio – we are drawn to it like paperclips to a magnet.

It's not surprising then that water has been an extremely important element in gardens since the earliest times, and not just for the obvious practical purpose of watering the plants. In Persian paradise gardens, and the Islamic gardens that followed, pools and canals were symbolic of the wellspring of life, and of the belief that the world and paradise were divided into four quarters by rivers. In Chinese Taoist and Japanese Zen gardens, the presence of water is essential. It is one of the main life forces, and it is there to purify not only the body but also the spirit. If it is not possible for reasons of space or site to include the real thing, other than in a small stone basin or tsukabai for purification as you enter the garden, it is always represented symbolically with raked sand or gravel.

As we have become more and more conscious of our own gardens as a retreat from the world, so including water in them has become increasingly important.

STILL WATER

The sight of water is a wonderful aid to relaxation and contemplation. A still pool, even a shallow bowl in the tiniest space, makes a mirror for the sky, reflecting the sun and the ever-changing patterns of the clouds, and bringing light down into the garden. By using a black pond liner, or painting the inside of the pool black, you can make even 30cm (1ft) of water suggest infinite depths. Staring into it takes your

mind out of the garden and the day-to-day world, and lets it roam free.

If you like you can add plants to the pool – choose something suitable for the size – and even a few fish, which are fascinating to watch. You'll find, too, that no matter how small the pond, within hours of it being filled, wildlife will start to arrive – damsel- and dragonflies, pond skaters and, if the season is right, frogs and newts. They all add to the show as well as giving you the satisfaction of being plugged into the natural world and of doing your bit for the planet.

MOVING WATER

Moving water has a different fascination. A stream burbling through and over pebbles provides an ever-changing display, and yet from a practical point of view in the garden, you only need a depth of an inch or two to create the illusion of a deep, fast-flowing current. A fountain in a pond throws droplets of water in the air which are refracted by the sunlight to make mini-rainbows before falling back first to pit the surface and then to create ripples across it. If there is no space for a pool, and for safety reasons standing water isn't a good idea, then try a bubble fountain. This sends water gurgling up from a concealed reservoir to trickle out through a pile of cobbles or, for more a more modern look, iridescent glass florists' nuggets, a shallow stone basin with a hole in the bottom, or if the budget runs to it, a large glass sphere. A wall fountain is another option, especially if you only have a balcony or roof terrace, and the terracotta or ceramic kind that are completely self-contained are ideal.

Any moving water in the garden gives you that other great asset – sound. We respond to the sound of water in a very elemental way, perhaps because the first sounds we ever heard were swooshing and gurgling ones. Providing it's not too loud, it can be very soothing and relaxing and, while it can't wipe out the noises of everyday life – it would take a miniature Niagara Falls to do that – it can distract you sufficiently for you not to notice them any more. On a hot day, the sound of running water makes you feel cooler. Certainly droplets of water do actually cool the air down but the psychological effect of the sound magnifies the cooling effect.

To an extent you can control the noise the water makes. Simply adjusting the flow valve on your pump can make the splashing louder or softer. If you have a wall fountain spurting a jet of water into a pool or bowl below, and you want a more muted sound, borrow an idea from the Japanese and lay bamboo canes across the top to break up the jet. By adjusting the position of the canes you can create different sounds.

HOW WATER IS GOOD FOR YOU

The sight and sound of water in the garden not only refreshes the mind and the spirit, it also refreshes the body because water droplets ionize the air. Ions are particles in the air which carry an electrical charge and according to whether they have gained or lost an electron they are either positive or negative. You might expect the positive ions to be the good guys, but in fact they are the ones that in excess make you feel lethargic, lacking in energy and give you headaches. Negative ions are the good guys and have been described as the 'vitamins of the air'. They increase the amount of oxygen carried round the body in the bloodstream and taken up by the cells, while positive ions deplete it. They attach themselves to pollutants in the atmosphere

and 'ground' them, but in the process they lose their electrical charge and are neutralized. That is why air on a busy city street contains only 200 negative ions per cubic centimetre when the norm is 1000 (with 1200 positive ions) and pure mountain air contains 10,000. In sealed, air-conditioned office buildings it can be as low as 20 – a major factor perhaps in 'sick building syndrome'.

Negative ions are produced by electrical activity, as in thunderstorms – that's why the air always feels fresher after a storm – and also by water breaking into minute droplets. So obviously they are produced in large quantities close to

Even the smallest garden can find room for a water feature. A jet throwing the water into the air increases the number of beneficial negative ions.

water. That's why we feel better at the seaside, or by a river. The air feels fresh, what we describe as 'bracing', and we feel invigorated.

In a small way, including moving water in your garden can help redress the balance. A fountain is probably best because it throws water straight up into the air, but any activity that will release droplets is fine.

WATER IN THE HEALING GARDEN

In the healing garden we wanted the best of both worlds – moving and still water. Since we wanted to divide the garden into two very distinct areas, water seemed to be the best way to do to it. There is something very deliberate and symbolic about crossing water – leaving the past behind and reaching – if it doesn't sound too fanciful – some sort of promised land.

Designer Jean Goldberry decided on a diagonal rill across the whole width of the garden, with raised beds at either end. It is 45cm (18in) across and 30cm (12in) deep. To keep the sides rigid, we built walls on

each side with railway sleepers, the tops of which formed the edging to the rill. It was then lined with a butyl liner. It's always slightly tricky in an angular pond to lose the surplus liner at the corners. The easiest way to do it is to half-fill the pond with water to weigh it down and stretch it out and then you can fold the surplus as neatly as you can. To finish off the rill, we used stout rope that looks like hemp but is in fact man-made so that it wouldn't shrink or rot. This was nailed over the liner at the very top, so that the rope finished flush with the top edge of the sleeper. It needs to be nailed every 10cm (4in) or so, and the neatest way is to untwist the rope, push the nail in, hammer it home, and then let the rope twist up again, so hiding the nail. To help disguise the inevitable bunching in the corners, we tied big, loose knots, and hid the cut ends behind one of them. Once the rope was in place, we cut away the excess liner with a sharp craft knife as close to the rope as possible. With the water up to the bottom of the rope, you couldn't see any liner at all. Inevitably, wildlife found it very quickly and with a week or two it had acquired its resident frog.

The rill was our still water feature and since we wanted it to be reflective, we left it unplanted. To give us moving water, at one end we placed a large black fibreglass sphere, slightly smaller in diameter than the width of the rill, so that it fitted neatly. Water was pumped up through the hollow centre to bubble out of the top and spill over the sides, making a gentle gurgling sound. It was carefully positioned so that you see it as you're standing at the kitchen sink with the blue bed behind it.

WATER IN YOUR GARDEN

There could hardly have been a better time to create a water feature in your garden. There are so many products available to make it simple to do, and so many different ideas on offer in magazines, books and television programmes that you really are spoilt for choice.

An electrician fitted a power supply in the garden to operate both the pump and the ultra-violet filtration unit, installed at the back of the rill to keep the water free from algae. If you're not going to have plants in a water feature, it's the only way. You cross the rill by means of stepping stones made from triangular wooden boxes filled with white cement, into which were set large, iridescent bubble marbles.

The first thing to do is decide what style of water feature, or features – no reason why you can't have more than one – would work best in your garden. If you have an informal cottage garden then an informal pond would be best, one that looks as natural as possible. The best way to make it is with a butyl or PVC liner rather than with a pre-formed fibreglass or plastic mould, which always looks artificial. Using

The rill, marble stepping stones and sphere in the healing garden.

Ponds always act as a magnet, not just for wildlife but for people as well. This formal pool at the bottom of the garden draws people down there to look into it.

a liner gives you the opportunity to dig out a natural-looking shape, one with sweeping gentle curves rather than lots of fiddly little ones. If you plan to put fish in it, it will need to be at least 60cm (2ft) deep in the centre to protect them in winter if the pond freezes over. Make a shelf about 30cm (1ft) down on which to stand marginal plants in baskets. This still looks natural, but prevents any plants get-ting over-ambitious and makes it much easier to divide them up if they do.

To maintain the natural look, it's important to hide the liner. If the pool is adjoining a lawn, a couple of rows of turf is probably easiest. If it's surrounded by planting, then try using turf laid upside-down. That may sound odd but the roots of the turf hold the soil into which they are growing in place and stop it falling into the water until it settles and melds together with the surrounding soil.

Formal water features

A more formal garden, or a patio, calls for a more formal water feature. This can be built into the patio if you are laying a new

one and a simple geometric shape works best – a square, rectangle or circle. On an existing patio, think about building a raised pond. The inside can be rendered with a special waterproof render and sealed with pond paint – black for the best reflections or a natural stone colour. Don't forget to build in a duct to take the cable for a pump. Finish off the pool with a broad coping round the top so that you can sit on it, and look down into the water. If you have very small children and safety is a factor, think about a bubble fountain. You could lift a couple of slabs on the patio and dig out a hole large enough to take the reservoir. If you buy a bubble fountain kit, it comes with a lid, but if you wanted to be sure no one could put a foot through it, use a piece of stout metal grid instead. Pile cobbles on top or a large stone, drilled through the centre so that the water can bubble up through it and spill over the sides, or a millstone –reconstituted stone or fibreglass – or a more modern material (see page 151). Or think about a wall fountain. This doesn't have to be a lion or Green Man mask. It could be an abstract structure with, say, a series of bowls interlinked so that the water travels from one to the other, side to side on its way down. This could be ceramic, treated wood or metal. Or you could create a waterfall by pumping the water up to a horizontal pipe fixed high on the wall and pieced with a row of small holes. If you want something unusual, contact a local craftsman. If you don't know one, try getting in touch with your local art college. You may find a student there who could create something unique for you.

Water streaming from the bold bronze lips of the sculpture flows down through several levels, creating a gentle, soothing sound which masks noise from the outside world.

Houttuynia cordata 'Chamaeleon'

PLANTS FOR YOUR WATER FEATURE

FS = flowering season

H&S = average height and/or spread given at 2–3 years

D = depth of water

Whatever else you choose for aesthetic reasons, you will need oxygenating plants to keep the water healthy. *Elodea crispa* is probably the most widely available. You can simply throw little pieces weighted down with lead into the pond, but it is very vigorous, so you're better off planting it in baskets where you can more easily control its rampageous tendencies. Alternatively try hornwort (*Ceratophyllum demersum*) or the native whorled water milfoil (*Myriophyllum verticillatum*). But avoid like the plague its South American cousin, parrot's feather (*Myriophyllum aquaticum*). This is very invasive and having escaped into the wild is clogging our rivers and canals at an alarming rate.

Deep-water plants

Aponogeton distachyos (Water hawthorn)

FS Mar–April, Aug–Sep. White, hawthorn-scented flowers. S 1.2m (4ft). D 15–45cm (6–18in).

Nymphaea (Water lily)

FOR LARGE PONDS

N. alba

FS May–Sep. Slightly fragrant white flowers. S 1.7m (5ft 6in). D 30cm–1m (1ft–3ft 3in).

N. 'Charles de Meurville'

FS May–Sep. Dark pink/red flowers. S 1.2–1.5m (4–5ft). D 1m (3ft 3in)

N. 'Gladstoneana'

FS May–Sep. Pure white flowers. S 1.5–2.5m (5–8ft). D 60cm–1.2m (2–4ft).

FOR MEDIUM-SIZED PONDS

N. 'Escarboucle'

FS May–Sep. Vermilion flowers. S 1.2 m (4ft). D 30–60cm (1–2ft).

Lysichiton americanus (American skunk cabbage)

N. 'Gonnère'
FS May–Sep. White scented flowers. S 90cm–1.2m (3–4ft). D 50–75cm (1ft 8in–2ft 6in).

N. 'Marliacea Carnea'
FS May–Sep. Pink flowers. S 1.2m (4ft). D 30–45cm (1ft–1ft 6 in).

N. 'Marliacea Chromatella'
FS May–Sep. Yellow flowers. S 1.2m plus (4ft plus). D 30–45cm (1–1ft 6 in).

FOR SMALL PONDS
N. 'Pygmaea Helvola'
FS May–Sep. Yellow flowers. S 25–40cm (10–16in). D 15–25cm (6–10in).

N. odorata var. minor
FS May–Sep. White scented flowers. S 1m (3ft). D 15–25cm (6–10in).

N. tetragona
FS May–Sep. Slightly fragrant white flowers. S 25–40cm (10–16in). D 15–25cm (6–10in).

Marginals
Acorus calamus 'Variegatus'
(Sweet rush)
Tall sword-like leaves, striped with cream. H&S 60 × 60cm (2 × 2ft). D 22cm (9in).

Caltha palustris (Marsh marigold or kingcup)
FS Mar–May. Golden flowers. H&S 22–40 × 45cm (9–16 × 18in). D 22cm (9in).

Cyperus papyrus (Papyrus)
FS Jun–Sep. Very tall, slender stems with mopheads of very fine leaves and pale brown flowers. H&S 3–4 × 1m (10–12 × 3ft). D 0–25cm (0–10in).

Houttuynia cordata 'Chamaeleon'
FS Jun–Jul. White flowers. Bright green, cream and red variegated leaves. H&S 10cm × indefinite (4in × indefinite). D 0–5cm max (0–2in max).

Iris pseudacorus var. bastardii
(Yellow flag iris)
FS Jun–Aug. Pale yellow flowers. H&S 1–1.2m × indefinite (3–4ft × indefinite). D 0–15cm (0–6in).

Lysichiton americanus (American skunk cabbage)
FS Mar–Apr. Yellow flowers. Large green spinach-like leaves. H&S 1 × 1.2m (3 × 4ft). D 0–5cm (0–2in).

Myosotis scorpioides 'Mermaid'
(Water forget-me-not).
FS May–Jul. Blue flowers. H&S 15–23 x 30cm (6–9 x 12in). D 0–15cm (0–6in).

Pontederia cordata (Pickerel weed)
FS Jul–Sep. Blue flowers. Soft green, trowel-shaped leaves. H&S 75 × 45cm (2ft 6in × 1ft 6in). D 0–15cm (0–6in).

Sagittaria sagittifolia
(Arrowhead)
FS Jul–Aug. White flowers. Bright green, arrow-shaped leaves. H&S 90cm × indefinite (3ft × indefinite). D 20–30cm (8–12in).

Schoenoplectus tabernaemontani 'Zebrinus' (Zebra rush)
FS Jun–Jul. Insignificant brown flowers. Slender, pencil-like leaves,

Typha minima (Miniature bulrush)

with horizontal white stripes. E. H&S 1m × 60cm (3ft 3in × 2ft). D 7.5–12.5cm (3–5in).

Typha minima (Miniature bulrush)
FS Jul–Aug. Insignificant brown flowers followed by characteristic cylindrical brown seedheads. Long, slim, rush-like leaves. H&S 45–60 × 30cm (1ft 6in–2ft × 1ft). D 0–15cm (0–6in).

Zantedeschia aethiopica 'Crowborough' (Arum lily)
FS Jun–Sep. Large white flowers, with central yellow spike. H&S 60–90 × 45cm (2–3ft × 18in).

Low-allergen gardens

This book is about the many ways that gardening and gardens can be good for you, but we mustn't forget that for some people – well over ten million of them – far from being a healing experience, they can be the cause of major health problems. For them, a short walk round the garden can result in coughing or wheezing, painful shortness of breath, sore throats, runny noses, sneezing fits, red, sore, swollen or itchy eyes.

Iris sibirica 'Sea Shadows'

They are the ten million people in Britain who suffer from hay fever, which affects the nose and eyes, and the three million (and rising fast) people who suffer from asthma, which affects the lungs and airways. Some people are unlucky enough to suffer from both.

The cause of these allergic reactions in most cases is pollen, from the flowers of trees in the spring, grass or other plants in the summer or, sometimes in autumn, weeds and fungal or mould spores from decaying vegetation, either in compost heaps or even just on the soil where plants have died and started to rot. In some cases, strong fragrance can also trigger attacks of asthma and hay fever, which should come as no surprise given how powerful an effect scent has on the body and brain (see page 119).

Some people are allergic only to a certain scent or pollen – grass for example, which is why they suffer most in June or July – while others are allergic to the whole lot.

Lawns are a major potential hazard for hay fever sufferers, so opt for some attractive hard landscaping instead. Using trellis to replace hedges eliminates another possible source of allergens.

An allergic reaction to plants shows itself in other people as a skin condition – eczema, urticaria, which looks like nettle rash, contact dermatitis, or photodermatitis where it is the combination of sunlight and the plant's sap which causes the reaction. Rue (*Ruta graveolens*) and giant hogweed are among the main culprits here and can cause very painful chemical burns.

While nobody enjoys being stung by a bee or a wasp, a comparatively small number of people have a severe allergic reaction to such stings, so severe in fact that in a small number of cases it can prove fatal. Obviously if anyone in your family has such an allergic reaction, it makes sense to avoid any plants that attract bees, such as thyme and buddleia (check a wildlife gardening book for a comprehensive list of bee-attracting plants). Also, remove any fruit trees to which wasps will be drawn.

The good news is that with careful planning you can create a garden that excludes

Passionflower and a non-scented clematis (*C.* 'Multi Blue') are suitable climbers for a low-allergen garden.

or at least minimizes the potential allergens, and allows you and your family to enjoy the many benefits that gardens and gardening can bring. After all, it seems such a shame that so many people have to spend the warm summer months shut up indoors.

Garden designer Lucy Huntingdon, who has designed a number of low-allergen gardens, many in association with the British Asthma Campaign, believes that the most important first step is to find out exactly which allergens are causing the problem. Ask your doctor to send you, or whoever in the family is the sufferer, for some tests. It may be that you are allergic to only one particular type of pollen or mould. If so, it would be relatively straightforward to exclude the plants responsible from your garden.

If the problem is more generalized, though, you will need to rethink your whole garden.

LOSING THE LAWN

The first thing to consider is the lawn. You may not think of grass as a flowering plant, but it is, and, for the majority of hay fever sufferers, grass pollen is one of the major triggers. It also harbours at its base pollen grains from other plants and fungal spores, which fly up every time the grass is mown. Indeed, some people also get a painful rash from pieces of flying grass, which is why you should always mow in long trousers, long-sleeved top and stout shoes, not flip-flops and shorts. For all these reasons, it makes sense to get rid of the lawn.

In a small garden, that is really not a major problem, and from both a design and practical point of view it's often the best solution even where no one suffers from any allergies. Many people, I know, are initially loath to lose their lawns because they think the alternative is concrete fence-to-fence. But that is not true. You can replace it with an attractive mixture of hard landscaping – paving, bricks, cobbles, setts, gravel – and low-allergen groundcover planting, which will look much more interesting and attractive, will take less looking after, will stand up better to wear and tear than a very small lawn, and will be usable almost immediately after rain. If you really are wedded to a patch of green just to look at, think about a small thyme or chamomile

Right: A Japanese style garden, with the emphasis on hard materials rather than plants, is a good solution for allergy sufferers.

lawn, though for the latter make sure you choose *Chamaemelum* 'Treneague', the non-flowering kind, since the pollen of the flowers is allergenic. And be aware that until it is established it will involve quite a lot of maintenance in terms of weeding.

In response to parents who wanted a safe surface in the garden for children with allergy problems to play on, Lucy Huntingdon came up with rubberized tiles, which in the right colour look very good. The downside is that they are expensive and a few children, though nowhere near as many as have asthma, may be allergic to latex. Artificial turf – the proper stuff they use for football pitches – might be another solution, but again it is quite pricey. For something soft under swings or climbing frames, the material usually recommended, chipped bark, isn't suitable because of dust

California poppy (*Eschscholzia californica*) is a good choice here.

and fungal spores. Free-draining, non-staining sand – the sort sold for sandpits – is one option, provided you can find a way to keep the neighbourhood cats off.

In a very large garden, getting rid of the lawn is not so straightforward. For a start, it would be hugely expensive to pave it all and for another, it would look a bit odd if it were all hard landscaping, especially if you have a natural-looking garden with trees and woodland planting. The solution there is to prevent the grass from flowering by mowing regularly – at least twice a week in summer. While this would solve the problem of grass pollen, it wouldn't prevent other pollen and spores from being disturbed when the lawn was mown. The answer there is for someone who has no allergy problems to do the mowing and for anyone vulnerable to stay indoors until the job is done. Since pollen can travel a considerable distance, it would be worth explaining the situation to your neighbours and asking them to alert you when they're going to mow their lawns.

HACKING THE HEDGES

You also need to think about any hedges in the garden. For a start, many of the common hedging plants such as privet and box produce pollen to which many people are allergic, and the dreaded leylandii can cause dermatitis. Added to that, their dense, twiggy habit means that they harbour dust, pollen and fungal spores which, again, are released into the air whenever the hedge is trimmed.

If it's possible to take out the hedge, or if you are creating a boundary from scratch, put up a fence instead, against which you can grow low-allergen climbers, wall shrubs or just tall shrubs at the back of the border to add some living colour to the fences. Obviously, you don't want

A goldfish in a pond, no matter how small it is, gives a child with fur allergies the chance to care for a pet.

anything too dense or twiggy that needs regular pruning or it will create a similar problem to a hedge. Alternatively, make the fence an attractive feature in its own right. Stain or paint it an interesting colour – something not too strong that you know you can live with in all seasons – or decorate it with trellis or split reed or woven willow to make an interesting texture or an interplay between light and shadow.

If it's not possible to remove any existing hedges, do make sure that they are cut by someone who does not suffer from allergies, and that any sufferer stays inside while the job is done.

WATER

One of the functions a lawn has in a garden is to act as the open, still centre, setting off the planting around it. Water can fulfil a similar function. A formal pool, square, rectangular or circular, acts like a mirror, reflecting the sky and bringing light down into the garden.

A pool is an opportunity to keep fish too and while, as the old song says, you can't take a goldfish for walks, for children whose allergies prevent them having a furry pet, it is at least a chance to care for living creatures.

As we know from the previous chapter,

moving water, especially fountains that throw droplets up into the air, is beneficial for health. It increases the negative ions in the air which latch on to pollutants, including pollen grains, in the air and 'grounds' them. Another way to reduce the level of allergens in the air is to water the garden regularly – not just borders, but paths and patios, too. Obviously the water will disturb the air initially and send pollen and spores flying around, so ask someone who doesn't have any allergies to do the job.

LOW-ALLERGEN PLANTS

As for planting, the good news is that there are more than enough suitable low-allergen plants for you to create a beautiful garden. While the list of plants to be avoided (see page 169) may seem long, do remember that it's very unlikely that you or your family will be allergic to all or even most of them. That's why it is important to check out what your own individual triggers are before you start planning your garden.

There are plants of all types that are suitable for a low-allergen garden, from trees down to annuals. The one group of plants that ought to be avoided totally by asthma and hay fever sufferers is ornamental grasses. It's a shame because they are marvellous garden plants but, as always, there is a way round it. Instead, you can use plants with grass-like leaves to give you that essential vertical element – *Hemerocallis*, *Kniphofia*, *Libertia*, *Cordyline* and *Phormium*. Grasses are pollinated by wind rather than insects, and all wind-pollinated plants should be avoided because they produce vast quantities of pollen – necessarily since it's a far less efficient method than insect pollination. And being much lighter, this pollen is easily blown from plant to plant, and therefore far more likely to be inhaled. The main wind-pollinated plants are trees or shrubs that carry their flowers in spring as catkins.

One family of herbaceous and annual plants best avoided is the daisy and thistle family – now called Asteraceae. This includes Michaelmas daisies, and all other asters, *Anaphalis*, all chrysanthemums, corn-flowers, *Echinops*, *Calendula*, *Cosmos*, *Osteospermum*, *Helenium*, *Rudbeckia* and so on. Anything that has daisy flowers or ornamental thistles should be presumed guilty unless proven innocent, although some helianthus are now bred to be pollen-free.

Be wary of pinks (*Dianthus*) too, which are members of a family that includes not only carnations but sweet williams and *Gypsophila* too. Here, the problem is the very strong spicy scent, so either find a non-scented variety or avoid them altogether.

Weeds are also another source of allergens. Nettles, for example, fat hen, ragwort, docks, dandelions and plantains, which produce pollen from early spring right through to autumn, can be a problem for asthma and hay fever sufferers, as can members of the grass family – couch

The poached egg plant (*Limnanthes douglasii*) is one of the easiest hardy annuals to grow and is allergen-free.

and meadow. Many of these can also cause skin allergies, as can buttercups, greater celandine, giant hogweed, yarrow, scarlet pimpernel and shepherd's purse. If you suffer from asthma or hay fever, weed them out as soon they appear and before they come into flower. If yours is a skin allergy, make sure you are well protected as you weed. In both cases, once the soil is clean, mulch to prevent the weeds reappearing as far as possible.

LOW-ALLERGEN GARDENING

If you suffer from asthma or hay fever, some times of day and some weather conditions are better for gardening than others. Avoid windy dry days where all the potential triggers will be blowing about. On still dry days, the safest time to garden is from around the middle of the day until late afternoon, avoiding early morning and the evenings. That's because the pollen grains rise high on thermal currents into the atmosphere during the morning as the temperature rises, and fall back as it begins to cool down, so the afternoon is the safest time. If the weather is very muggy and a storm seems likely, and indeed after a storm as well, it's best to stay out of the garden altogether, since the electrically charged atmosphere seems to increase the number of allergenic particles in the air. Autumn and winter, when there is little or no pollen flying around, are both good

Giving up grass is no sacrifice when the alternative is an attractive blend of different hard landscaping materials and trouble-free plants, such as the black grass-like *Ophiopogon* and silvery-green *Astelia chathamica*.

The delicate poppy *Papaver rhoeas* 'Angel Wings' is another easy annual that allergy-sufferers can safely grow in their gardens.

times to tackle major digging, though you may disturb fungal spores in the process, which can be a problem if you are allergic to them.

If you suffer from asthma, strenuous exertion in itself can trigger an attack, so learn to pace yourself, and if it seems to be a problem, then either get someone else to do the digging for you, or make yours a no-dig garden with lots of groundcover planting and, where practical, mulches. The most common forms of mulch – bark in all forms or garden compost or mushroom compost – are not suitable because of fungal spores. Cocoa shells also contain some fungal spores, but there are no reports as yet of any allergic problems. Gravel, or better still, weed-suppressing membrane topped with gravel for aesthetic purposes, is probably the best solution.

Compost bins are a potential source of problems, since they rely on fungal spores to break down any garden waste. If they are your trigger, and you are determined to make compost, use an enclosed system, get someone who has no allergies to spread it on the garden, and stay indoors while it's done.

People with skin allergies – or anyone tackling rue or euphorbias – should always garden well-protected. Wear long trousers, long-sleeved shirts and stout gauntlets to make sure there is no bare skin between shirt and glove, and even eye protection. It may sound excessive, but if euphorbia sap gets into your eyes it is agonizing, and can even cause temporary blindness.

Acanthus mollis (Bear's breeches).

Magnolia stellata

LOW-ALLERGEN PLANTS

FS = flowering season
H&S = average height and spread, given after 10 years for trees and shrubs, and after one full season for the rest
E = evergreen

Unless stated otherwise, you can assume that the plant likes a moderately fertile soil, neutral, moist but not boggy.

TREES

Amelanchier lamarckii
FS Apr. White flowers. H&S 6.5 × 5m (22 × 16ft). Sun/medium shade.

Arbutus unedo
FS Mar–May. White flowers. Fruit ripens Sep–Oct. E. H&S 2 × 2m (6 × 6ft). Neutral to acidic soil. Sun/light shade.

Crataegus laevigata 'Plena'
FS May–Jun. Double pink flowers. H&S 6 × 3m (20 × 10ft). Sun/medium shade.

Magnolia stellata
FS Mar–Apr. White flowers. H&S 1.5 × 2m (5 × 6ft). Sun/light shade.

Malus tschonoskii
FS Apr–May. Pink/white flowers. Yellow fruit ripens Sep–Oct. H&S 8 × 1.8m (26 × 6ft). Sun/light shade.

Prunus cerasifera
FS Mar–Apr. White/pink flowers. Purple/black fruit Sep–Oct. H&S 6 × 3m (20 × 10ft). Sun/light shade.

Prunus × subhirtella
FS intermittently Sep–Mar.

White/pink flowers. H&S 5 × 4m (16 × 13ft). Sun/light shade.

Sorbus aucuparia
FS Apr–May. White flowers. Red fruit Sep–Oct. H&S 5 × 2.5m (16 × 8ft). Sun/light shade.

SHRUBS

Aucuba japonica
FS Apr–May. Insignificant white flowers. Red fruit Sep–Jan. E. H&S 1.8 × 1.8m (6 × 6ft). Medium/deep shade.

Camellia japonica 'Mars'
FS Apr–May. Semi-double red flowers. E. H&S 2 × 2m (6 × 6ft). Well drained, moist acid soil. Light/medium shade.

Chaenomeles × superba 'Pink Lady'
FS Mar–Apr. Deep pink flowers. Yellow fruit Sep–Oct. H&S 3 × 3m (10 × 10ft). Sun/heavy shade.

Cistus × hybridus
FS May–Aug. White flowers. E. H&S 60 × 90cm (2 × 3ft). Full sun.

Cotinus coggygria
FS Jun–Jul. Pale pink flowers. H&S 3 × 3m (10 × 10ft). Sun/light shade.

Cotoneaster dammeri
FS Apr–May. White flowers. Red fruits follow. H&S 60cm × 2m (2 × 6ft). Sun/medium shade.

Escallonia 'Apple Blossom'
FS May–Jun. Pale pink flowers. E. H&S 3 × 4m (10 × 13ft). Sun/medium shade.

Forsythia × intermedia
FS Mar–Apr. Yellow flowers. H&S 3.5 × 2.5m (12 × 8ft). Sun/medium shade.

Fuchsia magellanica
FS Jul–Oct. Red/purple flowers. H&S 1.2 × 1.5m (4 × 5ft). Sun/light shade.

Hebe 'Autumn Glory'
FS Jun–Nov. Purple/blue flowers. E. H&S 50cm × 1m (1ft 8in × 3ft). Sun/light shade.

Hydrangea macrophylla 'Mariesii Perfecta'
FS Jul–Sep. Blue flowers. H&S 1.8 × 2m (6ft × 6ft 6in). Well-drained, moist, acid soil. Light shade.

Phormium tenax
FS Jul. Rust-red flowers produced on plants 4 years plus. H&S 1.5 × 2m (5 × 6ft). Full sun.

***Spiraea nipponica* 'Snowmound'**
FS May–Jun. White flowers. H&S
1.5 × 1.5m (5 × 5ft). Sun/medium
shade.

Viburnum tinus
FS Dec–Apr. Pink/white flowers.
E. H&S 2 × 2m (6 × 6ft). Sun/
light shade.

Vinca minor
FS May–Jun. Blue flowers. H&S
15 × 60cm (6in × 2ft). E. Sun/light
shade.

***Weigela florida* 'Albovariegata'**
FS May–Jun. Pink flowers. H&S
1.8 × 1.8m (6 × 6ft). Sun/medium
shade.

CLIMBERS

Actinidia kolomikta
FS May. Insignificant white
flowers. Edible fruit. White, pink
and green foliage. H&S 4 × 4m
(13 × 13ft). Neutral to acid soil.
Sheltered aspect. Sun/light shade.

***Clematis* 'Perle d'Azur'** (or any
unscented clematis)
FS Jul–Sep. Sky blue flowers. H&S
3.7 × 3.7m (12 × 12ft). Sun/light
shade.

***Hydrangea anomala* subsp.
*petiolaris***
FS Jun–Jul. White flowers. H&S
6 × 6m (20 × 20ft). Sun/medium
shade.

Parthenocissus quinquefolia
FS May–Jun. Insignificant flowers.
H&S 5 × 5m (16 × 16ft). Sun/light
shade.

Passiflora caerulea
FS Jul–Aug. Blue/white flowers.
H&S 4.9 × 4.9m (16 × 16ft). Shel-
tered position. Sun/light shade.

***Rosa* 'Mermaid'** (or any unscented
rose)
FS Jun–Sep. Single yellow flowers.
H&S 6 × 6m (20 × 20ft). Sun/
medium shade.

Vitis coignetiae
FS May–Jun. Insignificant flowers.
Berries ripen Sep–Oct. Not always
reliable. H&S 6 × 6m (20 × 20ft).
Sun/light shade.

***Vitis vinifera* 'Purpurea'**
FS May–Jun. Insignificant flowers.
Berries ripen Sep–Oct. H&S 4.6 ×
4.6m (15 × 15ft). Sun/light shade.

PERENNIALS

Acanthus spinosus
FS Jul–Aug. Blue and white
flowers. H&S 1.2m × 75cm (4 ×
2ft 6in). Sun/light shade.

***Agapanthus* Headbourne hybrids**
FS Jul–Sep. Blue flowers. H&S
1.2m × 45cm (4 × 1ft 6in). Sun/
light shade.

***Ajuga reptans* 'Burgundy Glow'**
FS Apr–Jun. Light blue flowers.
Wine-red leaves. E. H&S 30 ×
45cm (12 × 18in). Sun/full shade.

Alchemilla mollis
FS Jun–Jul. Lime green flowers.
H&S 30 × 60cm (1 × 2ft). Sun/
partial shade.

***Anemone* var. *japonica* and *A.* ×
*hybrida***
FS Aug–Sep. White or pink flowers. H&S 1.2m × 60cm (4 × 2ft).
Sun/light shade.

***Aquilegia vulgaris* var. *stellata*
'Nora Barlow'**
FS May–Jun. Pale green/red and
cream flowers. H&S 90 × 30cm
(3 × 1ft). Light shade.

Vinca minor

Bergenia cordifolia
FS Feb–Mar. Pink, white or red flowers. H&S 40 × 60cm (1ft 4in × 2ft). E. Full sun.

Campanula persicifolia
FS May–Jun. Blue flowers. H&S 90 × 45cm (3 × 1ft 6in). E. Sun/ partial shade.

Dicentra spectabilis
FS May–Jun. Pink flowers. H&S 90 × 60cm (3 × 2ft). Partial shade.

Geranium 'Johnson's Blue'
FS Jun–Aug. Blue flowers. H&S 40 × 60cm (15in × 2ft). Sun/light shade.

Geum 'Werner Arends'
FS May–Jun. Brick-red flowers. H&S 30 × 45cm (1 × 1ft 6in). Sun/light shade.

Hemerocallis 'Pink Damask'
FS Jul–Aug. Pink flowers. H&S 75 × 45cm (2ft 6in × 1ft 6in). Light shade.

Iris sibirica
FS May–Jun. Blue or white flowers. H&S 1.2m × 60cm

Dicentra spectabilis

(4 × 2ft). Sun/medium shade.

Nepeta mussinii
FS May–Jun. Mauve/blue flowers. H&S 30 × 60cm (1× 2ft). Sun/light shade.

Paeonia officinalis 'Rubra Plena'
FS Apr–May. Red flowers. H&S 1m × 75cm (3ft 3 in × 2ft 6in). Sun/ light shade.

Penstemon 'Sour Grapes'
FS May–Jun. Mauve/blue flowers. H&S 60 × 60cm (2 × 2ft). Sun/ light shade.

Pulmonaria officinalis 'White Wings'
FS Mar–Jun. White flowers. H&S 25 × 45cm (10in × 1ft 6in). Sun/light shade.

Rodgersia pinnata 'Superba'
FS Jun–Jul. Pink/red flowers. H&S 1.2m × 80cm (4 × 2ft 8in). Fertile moist soil. Sun/partial shade.

ANNUALS
Antirrhinum Madame Butterfly Series
FS May–Aug. Mixed double

flowers. H&S 60 × 30cm (2 × 1ft). Full sun.

Eschscholzia californica
FS May–Aug. Red, orange, yellow, pink, white flowers. H&S 30 × 15cm (12 × 6in). Full sun.

Impatiens walleriana
FS May–Sep. Mixed flowers. H&S 30 × 30cm (1 × 1ft). Full sun/shade.

Limnanthes douglasii
FS May–Jun. Yellow and white flowers. H&S 15 × 15cm (6 × 6in). Full sun.

Lobelia erinus 'Crystal Palace'
FS May–Sep. Blue flowers. H&S 10 × 15m (4 × 6in). Sun/partial shade.

Myosotis alpestris 'Blue Ball'
FS Mar–May. Blue flowers. H&S 15 × 15cm (6 × 6in). Sun/light shade.

Nigella damascena 'Miss Jekyll'
FS Jun–Jul. Blue flowers. H&S 45 × 25cm (18 × 10in). Full sun.

Papaver rhoeas
FS Jun–Jul. Pink, red, mauve, white flowers. H&S 60 × 30m (2 × 1ft). Full sun.

Petunia 'Apple Blossom'
FS May–Sep. Pink flowers. H&S 30 × 30cm (1 × 1ft). Full sun.

Phlox paniculata 'Mother of Pearl'
FS Jun–Aug. Pale pink flowers. H&S 90 × 45cm (3ft × 1ft 6in). Sun/light shade.

COMMON PLANTS TO AVOID

Plants marked **P** are also poisonous.

For asthma and hay fever sufferers

TREES
Acer (Maple)
Betula (Birch)
Carpinus (Hornbeam)
Corylus avellana (Hazel)
Fagus sylvatica (Beech)
Fraxinus (Ash)
Laburnum **P**
Populus (Poplar)

SHRUBS
Artemisia
Buddleia (Butterfly bush)
Ceanothus
Daphne **P**
Elaeagnus
Lavender
Ligustrum (Privet) **P**
Mahonia japonica
Olearia (Daisy bush)
Philadelphus (Mock orange)
Ribes sanguineum (Flowering currant)
Sambucus (Elder) **P**
Santolina (Cotton lavender)
Sarcococca (Christmas box)
Syringa (Lilac)

CLIMBERS
Clematis (avoid strongly scented species, e.g. *C. armandii* and *C. flammula*)
Fallopia baldschuanica (Russian vine)
Jasminum officinale (Jasmine)
Roses (avoid strongly scented varieties)
Solanum jasminoides
Wisteria floribunda (Wisteria) **P**

PERENNIALS — HARDY AND TENDER
Achillea
Asters (the whole daisy family, Asteraceae; see page 163)
Chamomile
Dahlia
Dianthus
Echinacea
Echinops
Erysimum (Wallflower)
Grasses (see page 163)
Lily
Lupin
Pelargonium
Persicaria
Solidago (Goldenrod)

ANNUALS
Ageratum
Arctotis
Centaurea (Cornflower)
Cosmos
Helianthus (Sunflower, see page 163)
Heliotrope
Matthiola (Stocks)
Nicotiana alata (Tobacco plant)
Oenothera (Evening primrose)
Reseda odorata (Mignonette)
Tagetes (French marigold)
Zinnia

For people with skin allergies

TREES
Ailanthus altissima (Tree of heaven)
Aralia elata
Ficus carica (Fig)
Juglans regia (Walnut)

SHRUBS
Artemisia
Cornus sanguinea (Dogwood)
Cydonia oblonga (Quince)
Daphne **P**
Fremontodendron Ligustrum (Privet) **P**

Lonicera × purpusii (Winter honeysuckle)
Rhododendron
Ruta graveolens (Rue) **Sap harmful to everybody**

CLIMBERS
Campsis radicans (Trumpet vine)
Hedera helix (Ivy) **P**
Humulus lupulus (Hop)
Lathyrus odoratus (Sweet pea) **P**
Lonicera japonica 'Halliana' (Japanese honeysuckle) **P**

PERENNIALS — HARDY AND TENDER
Achillea (Yarrow)
Aconitum (Monkshood) **P**
Alstroemeria
Angelica
Artemisia
Borage
Caltha palustris (Kingcup)
Dictamnus (Burning bush)
Euphorbia (Spurge) **Sap harmful to everyone**
Hellebore
Gaillardia
Leucanthemum (Shasta daisy)
Pelargonium
Primula (*P. obconica* is the most allergenic. Some newer varieties are non-allergenic.)
Pulsatilla (Pasque flower) **P**
Ranunculus **P**

ANNUALS
Amaranthus (Love-lies-bleeding)
Calendula (Pot marigold)
Argyranthemum (Marguerite)
Cleome hassleriana (Spider flower)
Erysimum (Wallflower)
Lantana **P**
Nicotiana (Tobacco plant)
Ricinus (Castor oil plant) **P**
Senecio cineraria

Afterword

As a result of researching and writing this book, I have found that I have started to look at my garden in a slightly different way. It has always given me great pleasure, but now that I understand a little more about the reasons why, I find I enjoy it even more than before.

Even small changes I have made as a result have made a big difference. Pushing an old garden bench back into a row of arching *Phyllostachys nigra* so that I now sit within a green cave that rustles gently in the slightest breeze, has created an ideal place to relax with a cup of tea and survey the garden, or even just sit and switch off.

Certainly it will affect the way I garden in future. Scent will be more important in my choice of plants, and what will dictate my choice of colours won't simply be the fact that I like them.

I hope that this book will have a similar effect on you, and that even if you don't make any changes to your garden or your gardening, you will get even more enjoyment from both than you do already.

ACKNOWLEDGEMENTS

Grateful thanks to Stefan Ball, Judy Howard, Theo Gimbel, Anne McIntyre, Barbara Payne and Betty Talks for sharing their knowledge with me, though any errors are all my own work. A special thank you to the late Amanda Metcalf of Artplace, who understood the healing power of beauty, whether in gardening or in art, and who was the inspiration behind Worthing Hospital's healing garden. Thanks too, to Steve and Liz Newman for letting us loose in their garden, and especially to the Catalyst Television team that made *The Healing Garden* possible – the film crew Gerry Dawson and Pete Jones, and the production team Mandy Bishop, Len Kerswill and Marisa Merry. And, as always, to Tony without whom…

SUPPLIERS

The following suppliers provided materials for *The Healing Garden*: M. Benson Contracting (01494 758147), B&Q Warehouses (02380 256256), Bradshaws Direct (01904 691169), British Waterways (01923 208700), The Chimenea Company (01923 261111), Cuprinol Ltd (01373 475000), Gem Gardening (01254 356635), HSS Hire Shops (0845 728 2828), Jekka's Herb Farm (01454 418878), Jewson Ltd (0800 539766), Marshalls Building Products (01422 306300), Oasis (01342 716111), Olympic (01737 789023), Rugby Cement (01788 542111), The Scrap Store (01803 524666), Sunshine Garden Products Ltd (01420 511500), Timber Decking Association (01977 679812), Wolf Garden (01495 306600), Wood Lodge Products (01932 223412), W.R. Outhwaite & Son Ropemakers (01969 667487).

PICTURE CREDITS

BBC Worldwide would like to thank the following for providing photographs and for permission to reproduce copyright material. While every effort has been made to trace and acknowledge all copyright holders, we would like to apologise should there be any errors or omissions.

All photographs copyright Jonathan Buckley, except those from Ancient Art & Architecture Collection, p18; The Bach Centre, p134; The Bridgman Art Library, p44; The Garden Picture Library, p41; Robert Harding Picture Library, p16; Jerry Harpur, p32, p41 (designer Isabella Greene), p78; Science Photo Library, p88; Jane Vermeer/Woodfall Wild Images, p120; Jo Whitworth/BBC Worldwide, p143.

Jonathan Buckley would like to credit the following people: Belinda Barnes, Rommany Road, London SE27, p20; Richard Bird, Kilndown, Kent, p80; Declan Buckley, Petherton Road, London, p164; Noel Collum, Clinton Lodge, East Sussex, p61; Robin Green and Ralph Cade, Grafton Park Road, Worcester Park, London, p42, p91; Simon and Judith Hopkinson, Hollington Herb Garden, Berkshire, p46, p48, p54, p114, p117, p149; Paul Kelly, Church Lane, London SW19, p36, p161; Virginia Kennedy, Rosendale Road, London SE21, p22, p24; Rosemary Lindsay, Burbage Road, London SE24, p51; Christopher Lloyd, Great Dixter, East Sussex, p76, p85 left; Janie Lloyd Owen, Eglantine Road, London SW18, p118; Mrs. Macleod-Matthews, Chenies Manor, Herts, p126; Jackie McLaren, Westwood Park, London SE23, p26; Bob Parker, Broad Lane, Wolverhampton, p162; Sarah Raven, Perch Hill, East Sussex, p113; Nick Ryan, Culverden Road, London SW12, p158; John Sarbutt, Grosvenor Park, London SE25, p152; Gay Search (design: Dan Pearson), London SW13, p90, p95; David Seeney, Upper Mill Cottage, Kent, p31; Susan Sharkey, The Butts, Brentford, p47; Penny Smith (design), Sycamore Mews, London, p153; Sue and Wol Staines, Glen Chantry, Essex, p79; Alan Titchmarsh, Hampshire, p27; John Tordoff, Navarino Road, London E8, p23; Sarah Wain, West Dean Gardens, West Sussex, p93; Helen Yemm, Ketley's, East Sussex, p13, p129, p165.

BIBLIOGRAPHY

Stefan Ball, *Teach Yourself Bach Flower Remedies*, Hodder Headline, 2000

Theo Gimbel, *Healing with Colour*, Gaia Books, 1994

Sunniva Harte, *Zen Gardening*, Pavilion, 1999

Lucy Huntington, *Creating a Low-allergen Garden*, Mitchell Beazley, 1998

Anne McIntyre, *The Apothecary's Garden*, Piatkus Books, 1997

Anne McIntyre, *The Complete Floral Healer*, Gaia Books, 1996

Sue Minter, *The Apothecaries' Garden*, Sutton Publishing, 2000

Sue Minter, *The Healing Garden*, Tuttle Publishing, 1996

Donald Norfolk, *The Therapeutic Garden*, Bantam Press, 2000

Martin Palmer and David Manning, *Sacred Gardens*, Piatkus Books, 2000

Romy Rawlings, *Healing Gardens*, Weidenfeld Illustrated, 1998

WEBSITES

www.phytochemistry.freeserve.co.uk

www.herbmed.org

www.botanical.com

Index